working with groups on
family issues

structured exercises for exploring

- divorce • balancing work and family
- family problems • solo parenting • boundaries
- intimacy • stepfamilies

sandy stewart christian, msw, editor

WHOLE PERSON ASSOCIATES
Duluth, Minnesota

TABLE OF CONTENTS

EXPLORING FAMILY SYSTEMS

FAMILY HEALTH & DEVELOPMENT

FACING FAMILY PROBLEMS

© 1997 Whole Person Associates 210 W Michigan Duluth, MN 55802   (800) 247-6789

FAMILY & WORK

RESOURCES

INTRODUCTION

Much important family work occurs outside clinical settings—in schools, churches, community groups, volunteer training, support groups, family life education programs, college classrooms, workshops, retreats, and growth groups. And the reverse is also true—family education, growth, and support services are usually interwoven with traditional family counseling methods offered by marriage and family therapists in clinical settings.

When you work with groups on family issues, you typically have three choices for selection of process and content: adapt clinical material from family counseling books for lay audiences, adapt consumer-oriented self-help books to professional program needs, or create your own unique group process or model using a combination of resources. Few resources or handbooks are flexible enough to be easily adapted for use in *both* settings, by both clinical and nonclinical group leaders, for multiple purposes, depending on the needs of participants and group leaders.

Working with Groups on Family Issues is an attempt to bridge the world between self-help books and therapy materials and to provide resources needed to work effectively and efficiently on family issues in a variety of settings, with varying combinations of individuals, couples, and families. This book combines the experience, wisdom, and clinical know-how of experts in the field of marriage and family therapy with common sense and practical skills for coping with issues facing contemporary families—divorce, single parenting, stepfamilies, gay and lesbian issues, balancing work and family, and other special issues relevant to today's families.

Regardless of whether you are a teacher, trainer, therapist, consultant, counselor, pastor, social worker, support group leader, employee assistance coordinator, or program developer—working with groups on family issues is a challenging task. You have to decide on an appropriate balance between relevant cognitive and emotional material, self-disclosure and privacy, individual reflection and group interaction.

The boundaries between family education and therapy are not always clear. In reality, education and therapy both fall somewhere on a continuum of interventions designed to help people enhance their functioning as individuals, parents, couples, and families. On one end of the continuum, you might give a presentation using only cognitive information, without engaging folks on personal, interpersonal, or family relationship levels. At the other end of the scale, you might be leading a therapy group in which you invite people to explore their deepest feelings and family experiences in a group setting. The exercises in this book fall somewhere in the middle.

Each exercise is structured to include elements of cognitive and experiential learning. Most have a combination of didactic presentations or chalktalks, personal reflection or assessment, self-disclosure or interpersonal sharing, problem-solving, skill building, and planning. All were developed with respect for the rich diversity of modern families and firmly rooted in the belief that all individuals and families have strengths and resiliences that enable survival and growth in times of adversity.

There are twenty-four exercises organized into four sections.

◈ **Exploring Family Systems** includes creative, experiential processes for understanding family systems, learning about family of origin and current family patterns, discovering the power of family stories, and setting healthy boundaries in relationships.

◈ **Family Health and Development** gives participants quick and easy tools for exploring past and present family relationships from growth-oriented, developmental models, including a model for developing intimacy through play. Special issues of contemporary families are addressed: stepfamilies, single parents, gays and lesbians.

◈ **Facing Family Problems** focuses on discovering ways to break out of hurtful, unhealthy relationship patterns, finding new ways of responding to partners' emotions, taking responsibility for personal use of violence, developing rituals for divorce recovery, coping with family stress, and forgiving past hurts.

◈ **Family and Work** addresses the nearly universal stresses of balancing work and family; sorting out issues of gender, money, and power; building a shared vision between working partners; and finding ways to prevent family of origin dynamics from being repeated in workplace relationships.

The format is designed for easy use. You'll find that each exercise is described completely, including goals, group size, materials needed, step-by-step instructions, and variations.

☞ *Special instructions for the trainer are indicated by the pointing hand.*

● Mini-lecture (chalktalk) notes are preceded by a bullet.

✓ Questions to ask the group are preceded by a check.

➢ Directions for reflection sequences and group activities are indicated by an arrow.

Scripts to be read to the group are typed in italics.

Also included is a resource section which will give you ideas for expanding your knowledge about family issues and preparing workshops and presentations on some of the topics covered in this book.

In addition to following the usual professional ethics and standards for creating safe, respectful, and confidential group learning environments, we recommend using principles of *informed consent* when contracting with participants of your groups: tell participants exactly what you will be doing, what topics will be covered and in what depth, and the extent of self-disclosure and group interaction. Make sure that all participation is voluntary and based on clear information about your role and the role of participants.

Encourage people to think about possible ramifications of exploring family issues in groups, not only for themselves but also for family members who are not present. Because everyone is connected to one or more family systems, participant's insights, emotions, self-disclosure during group, and actions after the session are likely of have some effect—positive, negative, or mixed—on family, friends, or coworkers.

It is the group leader's responsibility to guide people through reflection about the consequences of actions taken in response to family issues raised in group and to encourage thoughtful, responsible, sensitive use of material presented in group. The first exercise, **Truth and Consequences**, offers a process for opening and closing sessions with reflections about possible effects of family work on self and others.

Working with groups on family issues carries some risks, but the benefits of promoting and supporting healthy family relationships are worth it because growth is contagious. Healthy patterns of relating can spread from person to person, family to family, community to community, and country to country. Let's give each other all the help we can in moving toward respectful, inclusive, nonviolent family and world cultures.

© 1997 Whole Person Associates 210 W Michigan Duluth, MN 55802   (800) 247-6789

exploring family systems

1 TRUTH AND CONSEQUENCES

This brief reflective exercise can be used before group sessions on family issues as a way of helping participants understand and appreciate possible consequences of exploring sensitive personal and family information.

GOALS

To consider possible consequences of exploring family issues, for self and other family members.

To think about ethical, responsible uses of sensitive personal and family information.

GROUP SIZE

Unlimited. Could also be used with individuals as part of screening or as preparation for group sessions.

TIME FRAME

10–15 minutes.

MATERIAL NEEDED

Blank sheets of paper.

PROCESS

1. Introduce the workshop topic or agenda, followed by a brief explanation or review of the way family systems work, emphasizing the point that all family members—regardless of physical or emotional distance from each other—are interconnected and can have a powerful effect on one another.

   ● **Every family is a system** with unique patterns that shape its individual members. Your family of origin (the group of people who comprised the extended family you grew up in) teaches you directly and indirectly how to respond to the outside world. The way you communicate, express feelings, develop relationships, solve problems, and cope with stress were probably shaped by your family system.

   ● **Systems by nature are always striving for equilibrium**—so any change is disruptive and threatening. Asking questions, challenging family rules, responding in patterns different than those of your family, and making other individual changes will upset the system in some way and will always have consequences, positive and negative, for you and your family.

2. Hand out blank sheets of paper and invite everyone to reflect on possible benefits of exploring their own family issues.

   ➤ Write down five possible benefits of exploring the truths about your family system, for yourself or other family members.

3. Invite participants to pick one of the five possible benefits on their list and share it with the large group in a quick go-around, generating a wide variety of examples from the group. Weave examples into a short chalktalk, summarizing possible positive benefits of exploring family issues.

   If your group is larger than eight people, divide into two or more groups for sharing. People who choose not to share examples can simply pass their turn to the next person.

   ● **Exploring family issues is part of your journey of self-understanding.** Self-awareness, insight, self-acceptance, understanding, forgiveness, improved communication, deeper and more intimate relationships, new skills, and emotional maturity are a few of the possible benefits of exploring your family issues.

4. Point out that exploring family truths is a powerful process that can also sometimes have negative or harmful consequences. Guide participants in a short reflection on possible negative consequences of exploring family issues.

   ➤ Now write down five possible negative or harmful consequences of exploring family issues, for yourself or other family members.

5. Ask participants to select one of the five possible negative consequences of exploring family issues and share it with the group in another quick go-around. Summarize examples shared by participants and weave them into a short chalktalk on possible negative or harmful effects of exploring family issues.

   ● **Telling the truth can have negative or harmful consequences** for yourself or other family members. Revealing your brother's homosexuality may have repercussions for his job security; confronting your mother about placing her first child for adoption may cause her to have a physical or mental crisis; telling the truth about your aunt's alcoholism may cause your family to turn against you.

6. Respond to questions or concerns raised by this exercise and then move on to the workshop topic or agenda, encouraging participants to keep issues about truth and consequences in mind today and afterwards, when they decide what to share with family members not present.

VARIATION

As part of the closing process, ask participants to revisit the same questions and make a new list of possible positive and negative consequences for themselves and other family members, based on what they learned in today's workshop. (Knowing what you know now, what changes would you make to your lists of positive and negative consequences of exploring family issues, for yourself or other family members?)

2 WHAT IS A FAMILY?

The dynamics of family systems come alive when people engage in this powerful role-play experience.

GOALS

To learn about family systems.

To reflect on the ways childhood family roles affects participation in an imaginary family.

GROUP SIZE

Works best with groups of 10 or more people.

TIME FRAME

50–60 minutes.

MATERIALS NEEDED

Ball of heavy string, cord, or rope (at least 100 feet); blank paper; newsprint; marker; horn, whistle, or harmonica.

PROCESS

1. Introduce the concept of family configurations by giving everyone a blank sheet of paper and asking them to draw a picture of their family of origin.

   ➤ Draw a picture of the family you grew up in, using stick figures to represent everyone in your family.

   ➤ Label each person (or pet) in your family with their first name.

2. Solicit from the group examples of their childhood household family configurations.

   ☞ *Look for nontraditional examples and supplement as needed to illustrate the vast diversity of families (divorced and single parent families, stepfamilies, adoptive families, foster families, extended families, etc.).*

3. Validate all family groups described, noting the variety of configurations. Then review the definition of a family and basic family systems concepts, allowing time as you go for people to reflect on their childhood family group.

☞ *Suggest that people keep their family drawings available for further reflection as you review the nature of family systems.*

● **The family is a small social system** comprising two or more people who have an *ongoing relationship*, commitment, or bond, *based on shared beliefs*, values, and rules, *for the purpose of nurturing each other* (affection, support, loyalty, etc.) and meeting basic needs (food, clothing, shelter) over years and decades.

Two gay men sharing a household and lifelong partnership are a family as are widowed sisters living together in a retirement community or a teenage mother living with her own parents.

● **A family includes all extended family members,** alive or deceased, near or far, past or present, who have an emotional influence on you. A mentally ill uncle or an alcoholic cousin may influence you powerfully; so might a brother or sister who ran away from home or was placed in an institution.

➤ Add to your picture the extended family members who had an emotional influence on you.

● **A system is more than the sum of its parts.** Every family has predictable patterns of interaction, and the behavior of every person in the group affects every other person in the clan. People assume roles in the system and get invested in each other's behavior, making interactions predictable over time. The system assumes a history and function of its own, like a baseball team with its unique playing rules (three strikes and you're out!) or code of behavior (chewing, spitting, and yelling are allowed).

4. Illustrate the concept of a family system with a group demonstration of a family and how it operates as a system. Recruit six volunteers for the demonstration. Give one of the volunteers a ball of string and explain how to use the string to create a visual symbol of a family network.

➤ Stand in a circle with eight to ten feet of space in the center.

➤ Begin by holding the end of the string and throwing the ball of string to the person standing across from you.

➤ When you catch the ball, hold onto the line of string at the point at which it will make a taut line between you and the person who threw the ball. Maintain your hold on the string while throwing the ball to another person, who in turn catches the ball, grasps the string, and throws the ball on to another person in the circle.

➤ Continue to throw the ball back and forth until everyone in the circle is holding the string at several different points and a unique geometric pattern has emerged.

5. Explore the system dynamics by asking individual members of the string family to try out different movements and positions you suggest and observing what happens to other people in the web (move closer, pull away, tug harder, drop the string).

☞ *Experiment with a few short scenarios and briefly process how people were affected by each change. Point out that all systems seek a place of balance, or* **homeostasis,** *which is what they saw happen when the string design took on new shapes.*

6. Resume the chalktalk on family systems concepts, inviting participants to reflect on their own families.

● **Homeostasis is the dynamic equilibrium that all systems seek** for stability. If family balance is upset by divorce, other family members (parents, siblings, or possibly the children) might step in to help run the family or fulfill the role of the noncustodial parent. Or if a parent is ill and unable to function, other family members might pick up the slack and help to "restore order." (Grandma takes over cooking and laundry.) Since most people get invested in keeping things the same as they were, these interventions often provide relief for all family members.

～ Write an example of how your childhood family maintained homeostasis by restoring balance to its system during times of upheaval or change.

● **All families have rules and myths.** A rule tells you how to behave: *don't get angry, keep a stiff upper lip, protect the youngest child.* Rules may be spoken or they may be unspoken, communicated nonverbally through actions and attitude. Myths predict what will happen if you break a rule: *if you get mad, you'll do irreparable harm; if you show your weakness, it'll scare the kids; if you indulge yourself in play, you'll become irresponsible.*

～ Write down one or two examples of rules and myths from your family of origin on your drawing.

● **Everyone in the family has a role** or function in the system. Perhaps your older sister never had to do household chores because her role in the family was to be *the beauty* (attract attention) or to be a *family hero* (bring success/fame/respect to the family). The baby might have the role of *everyone's darling* (we heap our love and kisses on the little one) or be seen as *the pest* (he gets into everything and breaks my stuff).

> What was your role in your childhood family household? Write one or two adjectives that describe this role beside the picture of you.

● **Families have essential tasks to perform.** The primary work of the family is to ensure that basic needs of its members are met, including food, clothing, and shelter. In addition, families need to provide a safe, caring environment where adults and children can give and receive affection and experience a sense of belonging and worth.

> What were your special tasks in the family system?

● **Families need healthy boundaries.** A boundary is a border, an imaginary fence or line of demarcation between individual family members, between subgroups within a family (parents/children, older/younger siblings, boys/girls, etc.) and around the family itself.

Parents might have boundaries like *knock before you enter our bedroom, don't interrupt a private conversation between Mom and Dad, keep our family business private from friends.* Kid's boundaries might include things like *our rooms are off limits to parents or siblings, personal diaries are private, curfew is 10:00 P.M., cuddling and kissing a boyfriend is okay, but intercourse is not.* Individual family members also need boundaries such as *I expect privacy in the bathroom, don't touch me unless I say it's okay, stay out of my dresser drawers, don't tease me about my curly hair.*

> Illustrate some of the boundaries in your family by drawing lines around family members, the family as a unit, or physical space in your home which represents these invisible lines of demarcation.

● **Families have a life cycle** and go through predictable stages of development with predictable stresses and strains. First, adults come together as a couple. In the early stages of intimacy, couples must sort out family of origin rules from their own values and goals. If they decide to become parents and children enter the family system, the couple faces the challenging adjustments of shifting to parenting roles and guiding children through school years into adulthood. As children leave the nest, parents have energy to reinvest in their relationship and themselves. Eventually, most families are faced with challenges of accommodating new members as children marry and have children of their own. They must also face the grief of losing members. Each stage brings special rewards and challenges, including positive and negative stresses associated with these family transitions.

➤ What life cycle transitions stand out to you as stressful for your family? Write an example of a positive or negative life change your family experienced.

7. Invite people to raise questions or share reactions to the material presented and when you have responded to issues raised by participants, move on to the experiential part of the exercise.

8. Announce that everyone will now have the opportunity to make family systems concepts come alive by working (or playing!) in small groups to create a fictitious family and live in this group for a brief time. Lead people through each step of the process, taking time to clarify questions and offer support for shy people.

☞ *Encourage people to take the risk to get involved in this exercise, but make sure that folks with strong reservations know they can assume an observer role in the large group and sit on the sidelines.*

➤ Stand up, walk around the room, and pair up with someone whom you would like to be in your family.

➤ When you've found a partner, briefly share your reasons for picking this person (*you looked friendly, you smiled at me, I was looking for someone older than me*, etc.).

☞ *Allow 3 minutes for this process.*

9. When everyone has found a partner (or formed a threesome, if there are odd numbers), guide people through a search for additional family members.

➤ Each pair should now scout around for another pair to add to their current family.

➤ When you have located your new family members, introduce yourselves and share briefly why you chose each other.

10. After the new family groups have established their tentative connections, instruct them to find an area of the room where they can pull chairs into a circle and sit down together. When groups are settled, explain the next step toward becoming a family.

➤ Take 5 minutes to decide what kind of family you want to be. You can be any kind of family you want, at any stage of family development: a single parent family, a stepfamily, a family with all boys or girls or no children, a multigeneration family, a happy, quiet family, or a troubled, loud family with wild teenagers. Create whatever you want.

➤ You each should decide on the role you want to play and the age you want to be.

- This is your chance to be whatever you want to be, to try out a role different from the role you played in your family of origin. If you were the responsible, good child, perhaps you want to be a rebellious teenager or a bratty six-year old; if you were the only boy in a family of girls, perhaps you want to try the role of daughter or sister.

➤ When you've decided on your role, give yourself a new name. Do not use your real name or the name of one of your actual family members.

☞ *During this time quietly check on the progress of each group, offer suggestions and support where needed, and be quick to remind people to avoid getting bogged down in details about their family situation.*

11. Check to make sure that each group has a beginning family identity and that everyone has picked out a family role, name, and age. Then give the go-ahead for small groups to begin their role play.

➤ Pretend that your family is trying to plan a birthday party for your grandmother, using this scenario as a beginning focus for your family interaction.

- Start interacting as a family and play out the role you have chosen. You will have 5 minutes to actually become the family you have just created.

- Don't worry about how well you play your role. Just do what comes naturally to you and have fun.

➤ Go ahead and start your role play. Keep the interaction going until you hear the signal to stop.

☞ *This is the moment when people will probably need extra encouragement because role playing can feel artificial and awkward. Keep reassuring folks to go ahead, be outrageous, laugh, yell, or whatever it takes to get into the play.*

12. After 5 minutes, interrupt the family discussions and announce that

it's time to get to know each family and learn what happened in their group. Walk around and briefly interview each family in front of the large group, using key questions to focus discussions.

> *To speed up the process, ask the family to select a spokesperson who will summarize family dynamics for the large group. Invite other family members to add comments if they want.*

> Introduce your family to the large group, giving names, roles, and ages of each family member.

> Tell us what your family was like—its style, mood, and patterns of communicating.

> What was the most surprising development in your family?

13. Summarize stories of family groups, incorporating family concepts discussed earlier. Use examples from role plays to illustrate how these ideas came alive in family interactions.

14. Invite participants to reflect on possible connections between the family of origin roles and their make-believe family roles.

> In your group family, take turns sharing insights and observations about the similarities and differences between the role you played (or play) in your family of origin and the role you played in your fictitious family.

> Share why you choose the role you did and what you learned from playing this role.

> You each have 2 minutes to share.

15. When 5–8 minutes have passed, invite people to share examples of their discoveries about the relevance of their childhood family role to this role-play experience.

> *Typically, people will start the role play with the intention of behaving very differently than they did in their family of origin and then be surprised to find themselves acting like themselves. This is an opportunity to make the point that family systems are powerful and it is natural to repeat roles that have been reinforced over many years.*

16. Invite participants to reflect on what they have learned in this exercise.

> Take a few minutes now before you leave to think about your family role. Record on your family drawing any insights you've gained.

17. End the session by praising everyone for having the courage to explore old and new family systems.

VARIATIONS

 Ask each family to make a family sculpture in *Step 12*.

 For an interesting and powerful demonstration of the effects of change in family systems, after *Step 12,* ask someone to move out of each fictitious family and instruct these outsiders to create a new family. Give each family a task related to this experience of change or loss, and repeat the process of *Steps 11* and *12*.

 Depending on the specific needs or issues of your audience, customize this process by specifying reasons that people have to leave the family (hospitalization for cancer or other illness, chemical dependency treatment, separation or divorce, etc.).

3 FAMILY MAP

This tried-and-true process for creating a visual illustration of family systems is fun, nonthreatening, and almost always helpful in demonstrating how family systems concepts are played out in an individual's family.

GOALS

To create a visual representation of family systems and related concepts.

To identify family roles, rules, and myths and explore their relevance to current family relationships.

GROUP SIZE

Unlimited. Can also be used with individuals.

TIME FRAME

30–40 minutes.

MATERIALS NEEDED

Newsprint; colored markers; horn or harmonica.

PROCESS

☞ *This process assumes that participants have had previous education or orientation to family systems concepts. It is an ideal follow-up to Exercise 2, **What is a Family?**, page 5.*

This exercise was written for groups of individual adults who may or may not be attending with partners or other adult family members. If you are working with whole family groups including children, modify the process by confining personal sharing of family maps to each person's family unit.

1. Unless you have just finished a presentation on family systems, briefly review basic family systems concepts, focusing on definitions of the family as a system, including roles, rules, myths, and boundaries.

2. Introduce the concept of a family map, using the metaphor of a road map, asking folks to brainstorm examples of the kinds of information they can get from a road map, and listing these ideas on newsprint.

   ☞ *Include overall size and shape of each state (family); locations or positions of towns (people in family); hubs of activity, distance between towns (individual family members); type of connection (weak, strong, turbulent, twisted, etc.); boundaries or borders between states (other families).*

3. Explain the concept of a family map further in a chalktalk, giving plenty of examples relevant to your audience.

   ● **A family map is a picture of your family system.** It is a symbolic, subjective representation of family relationships at a given moment of time. It may show you caught between parents' friction, banded together with siblings in opposition to parents, or tied to grandmother, the family matriarch. It may reveal how mother is the hub of the family, one brother is the center of attention, and another is on the outside of the family circle in the role of family rebel.

   ● **Family members will have different perceptions about family history.** The same events will be seen differently by each person in the family depending on a variety of factors such as age, role, and position in the family at the time the event occurred. If you were a toddler when grandpa died, your sense of loss will be different from that of your older brother who remembers wonderful fishing trips with him.

4. Lead participants in a short reflection to help them get focused on a period of time in their family that they want to map.

   ➤ Take a moment to reflect on a time in your family life that you want to explore.

      – First decide what family you want to picture: your family of origin or your family of choice.

      – Now close your eyes and travel in your mind back to a point of time that you want to examine more closely.

   ➤ When you know what period you want to explore, try to freeze this point of time in your mind so you can study it more closely and recall what was going on in your family at this time of your life.

      – Who was living in your household at this time?

      – What kinds of family interactions were typical of this period?

      – How close or distant were parents, brothers and sisters, and other family members?

      – Was there a lot of conflict between certain family members?

   ➤ When you have conjured up images of your family patterns at this time of your life, open your eyes.

---

5. Distribute newsprint and markers to everyone. Then give instructions for drawing family maps, showing people how to do it by drawing sample maps on a large piece of newsprint in front of the room.

> Now diagram your family system, using a circle to represent each person in your family.

  ~ Write each person's name by their circle, along with a one or two word adjective which describes that person and/or their role in the family (lonely, weak, strong, peacemaker, rebel, superstar, workaholic, worrywart, clown, etc.).

    Remind people to include everyone they consider to be part of their family, even if these people are not biologically or legally related (grandparents, neighbors, parents, best friends, foster children, uncle, landlord/tenant, dogs, cats, etc.).

  > Be sure to include yourself in the family map, and describe yourself and/or your own role with an adjective.

  > Place each circle in the position you think that person held in the family constellation.

    Prompt folks with examples: Father and son were so close they were intertwined; oldest daughter was cut off from the family; youngest girl was the baby at the heart of the family; mother and daughter were very close but mother and father conflicted; etc.

> Use lines to symbolize boundaries or the type of connections family members had with each other.

  > Use double lines to indicate close, positive bonds.
  ~ Use single lines to portray solid, but less intimate connections.
  > Use disconnected lines to show distant relationships.
  ~ Use jagged lines to depict conflicted, heated interactions.

6. After 6–8 minutes, interrupt people and invite group members to expand their family map by now reflecting on the rules and myths that were a powerful force shaping the direction of their family patterns. Briefly review definitions of rules and myths in a chalktalk.

  ● **Rules are the signs on our family map** telling us where to go, what to do and not do *(share and share alike; treat everyone the same; Dad gets first pick; boys count more than girls; parents must be obeyed without question; don't talk about feelings; no conflict allowed, put downs and fighting are the way to get what you want; don't air dirty laundry in public; do as I say, not as I do; work first, play later; do your best, always).*

● **Myths are beliefs or illusions shared by family members.** Myths are usually assumptions or exaggerations which stretch reality and serve the purpose of reinforcing family rules. For example, the myths that *happy couples do everything together* and *healthy families never argue or get mad at each other* support rules of pleasing others and not showing feelings, especially anger. Other myths might be *Dad is always right, nothing bad can happen to us, our family is perfect, we are a close family, honesty is always the best policy*, and *any conflict is destructive*.

7. Lead people through further reflection about the rules and myths in their family.

   ➤ At the bottom of your family map, list some of the important rules and myths that were a part of your family culture.

   ➢ Try to think of both spoken and unspoken rules and myths. Silent rules and myths were taught by example, not words. For example, you never saw your dad cry, and you picked up on the rule, *big boys don't cry*.

   ➤ Go ahead and add any final boundaries or other symbols you want to give meaning to your picture.

   ☞ *Allow 5 minutes for people to record their reflections.*

8. Initiate a process for people to talk about their family maps with another person outside their family.

   ➤ Find a nonfamily member whose hometown population was similar in size to your own hometown, using four categories: under 1,000; 1,000–10,000; 10,000–100,000; 100,0000 or more.

   ➢ When you have a partner, find a place to sit down together.

   ➢ Decide who will be **North**, and who will be **South**.

   ➤ **Norths** go first and share their family map with *Souths*.

   ➢ Tell why you arranged your family the way you did and explain the meaning of the labels and graphics you used to portray family relationships.

   ➢ Share some of your family rules and myths.

   ➤ **Souths** provide respectful listening and acceptance of *Norths* drawings.

   ➢ You each have 4 minutes to share your maps.

   ➤ After 4 minutes, when you hear the horn or harmonica, reverse roles so **Souths** can talk about their maps while *Norths* listen.

© 1997 Whole Person Associates 210 W Michigan Duluth, MN 55802   (800) 247-6789

☞ *Let people know when there is just 1 minute left before it is time to switch roles and then again when time is up.*

9. After 8 minutes, reconvene the large group and ask people to share examples of discoveries they made in drawing their family map.

10. Conclude with a chalktalk about how people can use their family maps as a visual aid for understanding—and possibly changing—the roles, rules, myths, and boundaries in their family relationships.

   ● **While you cannot change other family members, you can always change yourself.** Being able to see your role in your family and your position in the web of family relationships, you can ask yourself, "Is this where I want to be or how I want to be in my family?" If you're always in the middle between two people, you can make a conscious effort to disengage, using lighthearted humor or whatever it takes to get you out of the triangle.

   ● **Changing yourself will change the system.** If your role or response is different, the family system will have to rearrange. The nature of a system is such that a change in one changes all.

   ● **Other people might also want change.** Consider sharing your family map with your partner or children, or invite them to draw one of their own. Then talk about everyone's maps and see if other people want to change the picture. If you can all agree to work on improving one aspect of your family patterns, you're on your way toward rewriting the map.

VARIATIONS

▨ If you are leading a group for partners, have each couple pair up with another couple. Ask family members to become silent observers while their partner shares his/her family map with the other couple. This "eavesdropping with permission" might lead to interesting new discoveries about their partner or themselves.

▨ With preteens in family groups, drop the listing of rules and myths. Focus only on the maps that each person draws.

▨ To expand visual images of family maps, have people take turns sculpting their families in small groups. The sculptor appoints other group members to stand in for different family members, asking them to assume positions and postures symbolic of family roles and relationships.

4 JOURNEY TO THE CENTER

This powerful mini-workshop uses guided imagery, creative expression, and group sharing to explore early childhood and family of origin issues.

GOALS

To understand family of origin dynamics from a new perspective.

To explore possibilities of changing old family rules and creating a visual symbol to represent this transformation of self and family.

GROUP SIZE

Unlimited.

TIME FRAME

45–90 minutes.

MATERIALS NEEDED

Blank paper for all; cassette player and audiotape of soft nonintrusive meditation music; a comfortable room where lights can be dimmed; craft supplies: poster board approximately 18" x 24" for all, scissors, tape, glue, marking pencils, markers, material, magazines, buttons, ribbons, yarn, family photographs to cut out, nails, flowers, Band-Aids, gift wrapping supplies, and other odds and ends.

PROCESS

☞ *This exercise may evoke strong emotion and tears for some people but when sharing is done in a safe, supportive environment, people do not usually get overwhelmed by the process and can handle their feelings.*

1. Introduce the idea that family of origin issues affect current relationships by asking people to reflect on unresolved family issues. Distribute blank paper to each person.

   ➤ Write down an example of an unresolved family of origin issue or pattern that you believe is affecting your current relationships.

      ☞ *Prime the pump with examples: harboring resentment about an old childhood hurt; being too hard on yourself as a result of growing up in a critical, strict family; excessive competitiveness with an older sibling who could do no wrong in your parents' eyes, etc.*

2. Ask for examples of unresolved family issues, then invite people to engage in further reflection about their family of origin as you review nine common family dynamics.

> *Encourage people to take notes as they listen to the chalktalk. Pause after each point to allow time for writing personal reflections about family of origin dynamics.*

● **We all have unresolved family of origin issues and patterns.** Your family of origin experiences are part of you, so naturally they affect your current relationships. If old family issues are causing you to hang onto ideas about yourself or behaviors that no longer work, becoming fully aware of what has influenced you can help. There are nine main areas that are helpful to explore.

● **Developmental transitions**. Every family needs to deal with the normal changes that occur as people grow. For instance, teenagers need more independence from parents: later bedtimes and curfews. Developmental tasks such as these require flexibility in responding to the changing needs of everyone in your family.

> How flexible was your family in adapting to normal changes as people grew? Jot down a few notes about how your family handled transitions.

● **Differentiation**. The ability of your family to tolerate different opinions, ideas, and needs of others will tell you about its ability to differentiate. Differentiation means that your family had a tolerance for individuality so that children are not simply seen as clones of their parents.

> How well did your family members recognize and accept individual differences? Jot down some examples.

● **Boundaries.** Boundaries are spoken and unspoken rules in your family about how you should function as a family member, including rules about closeness, touch, privacy, autonomy, and other interpersonal codes of behavior. When boundaries are clear and healthy, they allow you psychological and physical space to be your own person with an assurance of privacy and safety.

> Write a brief description of your family boundaries. Were you able to be your own person in your family, or did others decide for you? Did you have privacy and safety?

● **Roles**. Every family has special interactional patterns held in place by roles. Your role in your family was used to fill special needs of your family, like a catcher on a ball team fills the need of the team for someone to cover home plate. Roles were assigned when you were young, when you had no choice about accepting or rejecting your family role. Your role might have changed over time or in response to new circumstances.

➤ What was your role in your family and how do you feel about it?

● **Family Secrets**. Secrets are real or imagined beliefs held by your family which may be known to some family members while unknown to others. Secrets may be held for generations, becoming myths over time. Common family secrets include the true identity of a biological parent, a teenage pregnancy, placement of a child for adoption, abuse, mental illness, or any other problems people feel bad about.

➤ Are you aware of any secrets in your family?

● **Family Myths**. Your family may have had spoken or unspoken illusions that were used to define itself to the outside world. Myths usually fall short of reality (family members presented a loving, *we're-one-big-happy-family* face to the world but fought like cats and dogs at home).

➤ Write an example of one of your family myths.

● **Rules.** Every family has unspoken directives that keep family members within boundaries, support roles and myths, and keep loyalties in place. A rule such as *don't air your dirty laundry in public* directs you to maintain family privacy, solve problems inside your family, and be loyal to the myth that *our family is perfect*.

➤ What were some of your family rules? What happened in your family when these rules were broken?

● **Rituals**. All families have rituals to smooth over life transitions, celebrate the new status or role of a family member, respond to unsolvable problems, and promote healing. Rituals can be an action with a particular topic or symbol (like a wedding ring), involving sensory experiences of touch, smell, taste, sound, or sight (kisses, flowers, cake, music, photographs), celebrated as a group.

➤ What rituals were important to your family? What rituals were missing?

3. Invite people to share comments or ask questions about the material reviewed. After you have responded to concerns raised by participants, move on to the meditation.

4. Introduce the meditation as an opportunity for everyone to revisit their family of origin, identify childhood family rules, and explore

possibilities of creating new rules, roles, and rituals that are more congruent with their true self or the person that they want to be.

5. Invite everyone to move around and find a comfortable place in the room for the meditation. When everyone seems to be settled, dim the lights, start the music, and read the **Journey to the Center** script.

   Read slowly and clearly, giving folks plenty of time to explore their images without having to rush.

6. Allow a few moments of silence before you announce the next part of the exercise.

7. Place the craft materials on a table in front of the room and invite people to recreate part of their inner journey using collage or drawing.

   > Create a collage or drawing to symbolize any part of your journey that you want.

      - Use any material you wish.

      - There are no rules or right things to make: whatever you decide to do is fine.

      - You have 10–15 minutes to create your collage or drawing, and then you will have the opportunity to share your creation with other people in the group, if you choose to do so, and ask for whatever support you might need from the group.

        Announce when time is half up, and then again when there are just 2 minutes left and it is time for people to put final touches on their artwork.

8. After 5–10 minutes, ask people to return unused craft material to the front and gather in small groups. Once everyone is settled, provide guidelines for sharing.

   Don't be surprised if this exercise triggers strong emotions.

   > Take 3 minutes each to show your creations to your group and share what you want about its meaning to you.

      - If you want comments, help, or support from others in your group, go ahead and ask for what you want.

      - It's okay to choose to not share your creation: Simply say, "I choose to pass" when it is your turn to share.

   > Listen attentively as others talk about their creation. If you are asked to provide help or support for another person, try to give it if you can.

> You each have 3 minutes of time in the spotlight, to use however you want.

> - The youngest person starts first.
> - The oldest person keeps time.

9. After everyone has had a chance to share their creations, reconvene the large group and invite people to give feedback on the exercise and what they are taking away from the process.

> *Some people may be feeling unsettled or disturbed by a new view of themselves or their family. Be aware of the extra support and reassurance these individuals may need.*

10. Give everyone a list of family/support resources in your community and conclude with a chalktalk about the ability of each person to change their self-concept and family role.

> ● **You have choices about your identity and family role.** Now that you are an adult, you can decide what roles fit and do not fit your true self. Just as you were able to modify your rules, roles and rituals in your fantasy, you can make changes in yourself a reality.

> ● **Use awareness of family of origin history** as you continue your journey to the center of yourself. Paradoxically, when you acknowledge and understand these powerful childhood influences, you empower yourself to change ideas and behaviors that were shaped by your family. By making these influences conscious, you are putting yourself in charge of your life.

VARIATIONS

> ■ If you are using this exercise with ongoing groups, ask participants to bring some symbolic objects from home and incorporate them into their collage.

> ■ Instead of making collages or drawings, give everyone a paper plate and ask people to draw a mask representing the face of their family of origin, illustrating the unique public face that their family shows to the world. Then ask people to turn the plate over and draw a picture of their true self. When everyone is finished, engage folks in a discussion about what they need to be themselves more fully.

> ■ To deepen the experience, spend more time in creating the collage (25–30 minutes) and in small group sharing (25–30 minutes).

This exercise was contributed by Madge Holmes, PhD.

JOURNEY TO THE CENTER

Find a comfortable position for your body . . .
so you can be completely relaxed.
If you find your mind wandering, allow it to listen . . .
as well as choose its own path.
Gently close your eyes . . .
Begin with a deep breath in through your nose . . .
all the way to the bottom of your spine . . .
and slowly let it out through your mouth.
Give a big sigh . . . you may begin to find your body softening and settling . . .
Breathe into the core of yourself . . . and feel the rhythm of breathing . . .
Still your mind.

Pause 10 seconds.

Imagine yourself on a path leading away from this room . . .
Allow your senses to come alive . . .
so that you are able to notice what you see . . .
hear . . . smell . . . and feel . . .

Pause 10 seconds.

As you walk in nature, you may see ahead a special place . . .
a place that is your safe place . . .
where you are in charge . . . and you decide who can come and go.
As you enter this age-old place . . .
be aware of how relaxed you feel in this spot . . .
Notice the sights . . . sounds . . . smells . . . and sensations you feel.
You may find a comfortable place to lie down . . . and relax.
Totally relaxed . . . just allow yourself to be in harmony and balance.

Pause 5 seconds.

Let the comfort penetrate your heart . . . and every cell.
When you feel rested . . . go back to a time in your life when you knew the world was okay . . . and you were okay.
Even if this means going back to a time before you were born.

Pause 10 seconds.

As you lie there . . . see the person you were . . .
when you believed in the benevolent universe . . .
Ask the person to come beside you . . . touching if you would like.
Tell that self all that has happened to you . . . since you last saw each other.

Pause 15 seconds.

Ask your young self to stay with you on the rest of your journey.
Experience the sense of safety being with that person . . .

  Pause 5 seconds.

Something draws you to a structure at the side of your safe place . . .
A home . . .
If you like . . . walk over to it.
As you get nearer . . . you may notice that this place is very familiar . . .
that you have spent time in this place.
Be aware of your feelings . . . as you approach the door.
This may be an opportunity for you to grow . . .
Notice without being involved . . .
Notice the sound of the house . . . the aroma . . . what you see . . .
the colors . . . textures . . . shapes.
Notice how you feel as you begin to explore this empty place . . .
first one room . . . then the next . . .
Notice your body . . . and your emotions . . .
Save your old bedroom for last.
Spend as much time as you would like in each room . . .
looking into closets and drawers . . . looking out of the window . . .

  Pause 10 seconds.

Go into your old bedroom . . . and if you would like . . .
put your head on your pillow . . . and lie a moment looking around . . .
You may notice some writing on the walls.
As you concentrate . . .
the writing becomes the rules that others have made for you.
One by one, go through each rule . . .
and check to see if each rule is one you wish to obey.
Continue to ask yourself if that is a good rule for you . . .
Does it work for you now? . . .
Have you outgrown it? . . .
Who created that rule for you? . . .
You may wish to use the eraser and pen . . .
to erase some old rules . . .
and create better ones for you.

  Pause 15 seconds.

Notice the family myths and secrets . . .
When did you become aware they existed?

  Pause 10 seconds.

If you are female . . .
ask your mother and grandmother to come into the room . . . and talk with you.
If you are male . . .
ask your father and grandfather to come and talk with you.

If you wish . . .
tell them about the new rules and boundaries you have created for yourself . . .
Watch their reaction . . .
How comfortable is your family when you redefine yourself? . . .
How able is your family to let each member grow . . .
and change as they age? . . .
Ask them to tell you about you . . .

      Pause 15 seconds.

Do you have any corrections?
With this new idea about yourself . . . go back into each room . . .
meeting a family member or important person . . . living or not . . .
and tell them about what you have discovered about yourself . . .
new roles . . . new boundaries . . . exposure of myths and secrets . . .
Tell them the ways your relationship may be changing . . .

      Pause 15 seconds.

Breathing deeply . . .
notice as you exhale that your breath may contain color . . .
Just pay attention to your breath . . . the color may change . . .
Notice the miracle of change . . .

      Pause 10 seconds.

Before you leave this house . . .
look for a symbol that represents your changing self . . .
or relationship . . . or something valuable from the past . . .
and put it into the pocket of your memory . . . to bring out with you.

      Pause 10 seconds.

Confer with your young self that came in with you . . .
Ask what was noticed about these old and current relationships . . .

      Pause 15 seconds.

If you wish, say good-bye to your room . . . your house . . .
and all the people that were there . . .
You may wish to congratulate yourself . . . for becoming you . . .
and feel gratitude about all that has shaped you.

      Pause 10 seconds.

As you walk back to your safe place . . .
contemplate what sort of ritual you wish to happen . . .
to celebrate your necessary changes.
If you wish . . . invite the people you need to attend . . .
You may call on the wisdom of your young self that knows the world is okay . . .

Remove the symbol that you are carrying . . .
in the pocket of your memory.
Place it out in front of you . . . and consider how you will use it.

          Pause 5 seconds.

Explain to the people gathered there what kind of ceremony you would like . . .
and ask for specific help or gifts . . . when you need it.
Remember that your ritual can be any act . . . or series of acts . . .
that help you move towards becoming yourself.
Pay attention to visual images . . .
sounds . . . tastes. . . smells . . . how things feel.
Just experience yourself.

          Pause 15 seconds.

Walk over to the special healing pool . . . at the side of your safe place.
Notice it is the perfect temperature . . . and immerse yourself . . .
washing away any unwanted thoughts or feelings . . .
Breathe slowly . . . and notice the color of your breath. Watch it change.
Feel the radiance of your personhood.

          Pause 10 seconds.

As you get ready to return to this room . . . decide what you will bring back.
Any symbols . . . rules about you . . . or your young self . . .
that knows the world is okay.
Whatever you wish . . . just shrink it down . . . and put it into your heart.

          Pause 5 seconds.

Say good-bye to your safe place . . . any people . . . any symbols . . .
knowing you can go back . . . just by closing your eyes.
Notice your body begin to stir . . . as you get ready to open your eyes.

Script written by Madge Holmes, PhD.

© 1997 Whole Person Associates 210 W Michigan Duluth, MN 55802   (800) 247-6789

5 BOUNDARY DILEMMAS

The day-to-day dilemmas that push us to define our boundaries are the focus of exploration in this fascinating, yet practical, exercise.

GOALS

To identify personal boundaries and limits.

To practice setting limits in relationships.

GROUP SIZE

Unlimited.

TIME FRAME

45–60 minutes.

MATERIALS NEEDED

Boundary Dilemmas worksheet.

PROCESS

1. Begin with a short chalktalk defining boundaries and the importance of setting them.

   ● **A boundary is something that sets a border or limit.** That border or limit can be physical, emotional, intellectual, or spiritual.

     ○ **Physical boundaries** refer to your body: your ability to control when and how others approach you, see you, or touch you. Refusing a hug from someone you do not like is an example of setting a physical boundary, as is locking a door on your bedroom, shutting a curtain on your window, and building a fence between your home and your neighbor's property.

     ○ **Emotional boundaries** have to do with your feelings: your ability to recognize, accept, and express your feelings, separate and distinct from those of others. When your emotional boundaries are well-developed, you—not other family members or friends—are in charge of your own feelings, moods, and problems. You can be compassionate toward others without taking on their feelings or problems and making them your own.

     ○ **Intellectual boundaries** allow you to have your own thoughts, ideas, beliefs, and values. You can speak for yourself, express your opinions, recognize ideas belonging to you, separate out ideas coming from other people or sources. When you assert your intellectual boundaries, you recognize and affirm your mental autonomy.

Spiritual boundaries refer to limits associated with your spiritual beliefs, customs, and values. If your spirituality carries the belief that Sunday is a day of rest, you honor this spiritual boundary by refusing to work on this day of the week. If altruism and service to others are an integral part of your spirituality, your boundaries may include involvement in a large, extended family network or outreach to strangers in need.

- **Boundaries can be spoken or unspoken.** Your actions, (walking away from a person who is insulting you) speak as loudly as your words (*I won't stand for this!*). Both can be effective ways of communicating your boundaries.

- **The purpose of setting boundaries is to take care of yourself.** Boundaries are ways to appropriately protect yourself, not create walls. Refusing to go rock-climbing with friends when you are not properly trained for this sport can be a lifesaving boundary. Saying *no* to obligations that make you miserable or cause you unbearable stress are ways to protect your health, not isolate you from people.

- **Setting a boundary means you respect yourself.** When you respect yourself, you protect yourself from inappropriate behavior. For example, you do not get drunk at a staff party or make a fool of yourself with your boss. By protecting yourself in this way, your self-worth is likely to remain high or grow.

- **Boundaries should be clear, specific, reasonable, and enforceable.** For example, you tell your boyfriend that you will go dancing with him at a local nightclub, but if he has more than one or two beers, you will drive the two of you home or take a taxi by yourself. Or you tell your son you will buy him a car, but he has to pay for his own car insurance, maintenance, and gas.

- **In healthy relationships, people respect each other's boundaries.** Each person respects the needs, values, thoughts, and feelings of the other, regardless how they differ from their own. When respect is reciprocal, the self-worth of *both* people will probably increase.

2. Invite questions about boundaries and clarify any misunderstandings about concepts.

3. Read one of the **Boundary Dilemmas** (page 31) and invite group discussions on setting boundaries in this situation.

   ✓ How would you handle this situation?

   ✓ What boundaries would you set, and how would you do it?

   ☞ *Solicit lots of options for setting boundaries. Remind folks there are no right answers.*

4. Hand out **Boundary Dilemmas** worksheets and form small groups of three or four people. When folks are settled, give instructions for discussion. (8–10 minutes)

   ➤ Read the boundary dilemmas on your worksheet and select two that you want to discuss as a group.

   ➤ Take turns identifying feelings you have about this dilemma, what boundaries, if any, you would need to set in a similar situation, and how you might go about setting them.

      ⁓ You each have 3 minutes to describe your responses to the two dilemmas.

      ⁓ Remember that your boundaries need to be specific, reasonable, and enforceable.

      ☞ *Also remind participants that appropriate boundaries are not threats, bluffs, violent acts, shouts, judgments, or moral evaluations. After 5 minutes encourage groups to move on to the second dilemma.*

5. When discussions of the selected dilemmas seem to be winding down, invite participants to reflect on their own boundary issues.

   ➤ Take a moment to identify one or two boundary dilemmas of your own—either situations you have experienced or situations you anticipate arising in the near future.

   ➤ When you have a dilemma in mind, leave your small group, move around the room, find a new partner, and sit down together.

      ⁓ Take turns sharing your boundary dilemma and your ideas for solving this dilemma.

      ⁓ You each have 5 minutes to share your dilemma and explore possible resolutions for it.

6. After 8–10 minutes, reconvene the large group and solicit examples of boundary dilemmas.

   ☞ *Hear from as many participants as time permits. To protect the privacy of everyone involved, remind people to speak in general terms and not use names.*

7. Summarize responses of participants and weave them into a closing chalktalk about the importance of resolving boundary dilemmas.

   ● **Every dilemma you face is an opportunity for self-care.** Boundary dilemmas are normal, everyday occurrences that can be viewed as choices about how to care for yourself as a whole person: physically, mentally, emotionally, and spiritually. Self-care grows from self-respect, and self-respect grows from self-care. Setting boundaries, when done respectfully, is a win-win situation, benefiting not only you but everyone in relationship with you.

VARIATION

▢ Ask participants to role-play the boundary dilemmas and to practice responding to them.

This exercise was contributed by Katherine Speare, PhD.

BOUNDARY DILEMMAS

Your spouse has been complaining about the condition of your mother's house. Your children go to their grandmother's after school each day. Your spouse feels that the atmosphere is chaotic and the home is dirty and would like for you to talk with her about it. You know she would be much more receptive to hearing it from you rather than from your spouse.
What are your boundaries? What do you do?

You are talking with your teenage daughter who has had a bad day. As you talk, she starts sobbing. Her sobbing is extremely deep and shows no signs of stopping. As you reach to hug and comfort her, she looks up angrily and says, "Leave me alone!" Your feeling are hurt.
What are your boundaries? What do you do?

You make weekly visits to the homebound members of your synagogue. You check on their overall well-being and make sure they have enough food and medicine. You have been asked to squeeze in a visit with a new synagogue member. She greets you at the door obviously having "dressed up" for the occasion. She invites you in to a table set for two with carefully prepared sandwiches, home baked cookies, and coffee. You're not particularly hungry and had planned to spend just a half hour there so you could have the rest of the day to yourself.
What are your limits? What do you do?

You have provided care for your aging aunt for eight months. She passed away two months ago, and you find yourself missing the company of having someone around on a daily basis. One of your good friends approaches you after church, saying that her mother-in-law is in need of care. She explains that she is too ill herself to provide the necessary care, but she and her husband would be glad to pay you for providing care for her. You can use the money and would love to see your friend more often, but you don't like her husband and her mother-in-law is rumored to be quite demanding.
What are your boundaries? What do you do?

At your job, you have become aware that a male colleague has been flirting with the new female staff member. She is a mature 32-year-old who is currently unattached. He, however, has been dating a close friend of yours for over a year.
What are your limits? What do you do?

You have been attending the same 12-step meeting for over five years. For the past three months, a person you know from work has begun to attend the same meeting. You have found yourself hesitant to talk about some of the concerns you have about your work as well as about the troubles you've been having with your teenager. You've tried a number of meetings over the years, but have found that this particular meeting is by far the best for you. Your sponsor also attends.
What are your limits? What do you do?

Your brother-in-law has been complaining of depression for several months. He is currently thinking about getting some antidepressant medication, but feels ashamed for being "weak" and not being able to solve his own problems. You have been taking antidepressant medication for some time. You know if you told him that, it would probably convince him to take the medication. At the same time, your in-laws, while well-meaning, have a tendency to tease and shame people about their foibles. Your brother-in-law has never been able to keep anything from the rest of the family.
What are your limits? What do you do?

© 1997 Whole Person Associates 210 W Michigan Duluth, MN 55802   (800) 247-6789

6 ONCE UPON A TIME

As people tap into the power of family stories, they begin to access memory and imagination, find their own voice, and rework family blueprints about who they are.

GOALS

To explore past, present, and future meanings of family stories.

To explore connections between family stories and family patterns.

GROUP SIZE

Unlimited.

TIME FRAME

50–60 minutes.

MATERIALS NEEDED

Family Tales worksheet; crayons or colored markers for participants.

PROCESS

1. Begin by asking people to share humorous family stories with other participants. (3–4 minutes)

    ➤ Pair up with someone you do not know well and share a short, funny story about your family.

      ➤ Pick one of your family's favorite stories or jokes, one that usually makes people in your family laugh in the retelling.

      ➤ You each have 1 minute to tell your story.

2. Ask everyone to be seated, invite folks to share examples of funny family stories or jokes, then give a brief chalktalk about the power of family stories to give life meaning.

    ● **We all have stories to tell.** Stories tell others who you are, where you came from, and where you're headed. They're like a river carrying your flow of meaning from past to present and future. You carry your stories with you, and when you tell them to others, they can become a powerful link bringing you together.

    ● **Telling your story is life-affirming.** Telling your story may enable you to find your own voice, bring forth silenced stories, and open up possibilities for new understanding of yourself and your family. Telling your story can give you life and offer you purpose.

● **We all want to be seen and heard**. It's human nature to long for the kind of honest intimacy that comes with knowing and being known for who you really are. The ability to be yourself, reveal your true self to others without fear of judgment or rejection, is a joy. When you think about it, the people you love the most are probably the ones who know your stories or unique life experiences and love you unconditionally.

3. Invite participants to explore past, present, and future meanings of a personal family story. Give everyone a **Family Tales** worksheet and some crayons or colored markers and guide them through each step of the process. (25–30 minutes)

> Close your eyes for a moment and recall a family story that has been passed down through the generations in your family.

   > When you have thought of a story, open your eyes and write a brief summary of the story as it was told to you in the cartoon balloon on your worksheet.

   > You have 4–6 minutes to write your story.

> Next recall *who* tells this story and *when*.

   > Write the name of the storyteller next to the cartoon character and the jot down a description of the circumstances in which this story is usually told.

      ☞ *Give examples (Grandma tells it every Christmas dinner, Jim always tells it when I bring a new boyfriend home, etc.).*

> Now focus on *who knows* the story.

   > Write the names of everyone who knows the story around the story balloon.

> Now reflect on the story itself and its messages for you and others in the family.

   > What are the different versions of this story? In the space labelled **Variations**, write some notes about how the story changes in different circumstances.

   > What feelings are conveyed by the storyteller when telling this family story? Write the feelings in the space provided.

      ☞ *For example, the story is told with feelings of joy, shame, humor, pride, mystery, sadness, etc.*

> What themes are embodied in the story? Write down any themes that you hear in the story.

> *Clarify the meaning of themes: they are the central point, meaning or message which runs throughout the story, such as, our family can survive hardship, never give up, love conquers all, laugh when the chips are down, etc.*

> What message does the story have for you as an adult? What does it tell you about what is expected of men and women and how you should view the outside world?

> *Give plenty of examples: Does it tell you to take yourself seriously or laugh at yourself? Does it instruct women to yield to men or seek equality? Does it portray the outside world as a friendly place or as dangerous?*

> How are you connected to the story? Are you a central character or a bystander? Is the story directed to you personally or passed on without discrimination to all children or grandchildren? Is the story connected to a significant event in your childhood?

> Write notes about your connection to the story, about the meaning or implications it has for you.

> Use crayons or colored markers to draw symbols, lines, arrows, or other indications of your story's meaning.

> Are there key people that you want to ask about the details of this story and/or their version of it? Write their names and the questions you would like to ask.

> When do you tell this story, and how do you modify it under different circumstances?

> *Prime the pump with examples: Do they edit the story when they tell it to their children to protect grandparents from having their weaknesses known to grandchildren? Do they change key facts to create a good impression or elicit sympathy and support from people?*

4. Invite people to share their stories and insights with a partner.

> Pair up with someone you do not know well and find a place to sit down together for storytelling.

> You each have 5 minutes to share whatever you want about your story: its meaning for you, any insights or discoveries you made by exploring your story in depth, etc.

> *Tell people that you will signal them when 5 minutes are up*

---

and it's time to reverse the roles so the second person can tell their tale.

5. After 8–10 minutes, interrupt the discussion and solicit examples of stories and insights from several different pairs. At appropriate points in the discussion, ask facilitative questions to promote participation.

   ✓ What have you learned about the power of stories as you've gone through this process?

   ✓ What similarities and differences did you discover between yourself and your partner when you shared your stories?

6. Weave participants' stories about what they have learned into a chalk-talk on the power of family stories and the universal need to be heard.

   ● **We all have stories.** We might dismiss them or consider them unimportant, yet when we start exploring their meaning for us, we discover that even simple stories can carry profound meaning for us—and our family. Stories convey values, philosophy of life, coping skills, successful mastery of challenging problems, historical connections to past ancestors, and more.

   ● **We all want to be seen and heard.** The experience of being listened to, known deeply, understood, and accepted by others is a gift. When we receive these gifts, we are honored.

   ● **Stories are life-affirming.** When you tell a story, you breathe life and meaning into an otherwise neutral event. You give a voice to your experiences and affirm the value of your existence.

7. Invite participants to join in a closing ritual of affirmation (3–4 minutes).

   ➤ Share with your partner what you appreciated about your exchange with them.

   ➤ Tell your partner what they did that helped you to feel seen, heard, and appreciated.

8. Close with an expression of your own appreciation for the stories shared here.

VARIATIONS

▦ Ask people to draw family genograms before reflecting, writing, and telling family stories. For more information about how to develop a genogram, refer to Monica McGoldrick's book, *You Can Go Home Again* (New York: Norton Press, 1995).

© 1997 Whole Person Associates 210 W Michigan Duluth, MN 55802   (800) 247-6789

▧ If people do not know each other well, start the exercise with discussion in pairs or small groups, using the following questions:

  ✓ What did you learn about listening and being listened to in your family of origin? in school? in other places? Did you notice differences in listening and being listened to for men, women, and children? If so, what differences did you notice?

  ✓ When have you really felt listened to, and what was happening that made you feel heard? When have you felt not listened to, and what was happening that made you feel unheard?

  ✓ Tell about one of your best listening experiences—what enabled you to listen so well? Tell about one of your worst listening experiences—what interfered with your ability to listen?

  ✓ Based on what you have learned about listening and being listened to, what do you see as your strengths and weaknesses in listening?

▧ Give out a second worksheet and ask people to rewrite the story from a new angle or perspective. Then repeat *Steps 3–5,* looking at how this new perspective changes the story's meaning or message. Invite people to share what happened when they rewrote their story from a new perspective, using this discussion as an opportunity to point out the power of stories to affect personal attitude, identity, family role, family rules, outlook on life, ability to cope with stress, etc.

Contributed by Janine Roberts. For more creative approaches to family systems education, refer to her outstanding book, Tales and Transformations: Stories in Families and Family Therapy *(New York: W. W. Norton & Company, 1994).*

FAMILY TALES

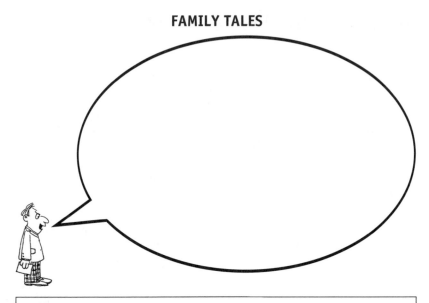

Variations
Feelings
Themes
Message
My Connections
Questions
Modifications

family HealtH & developmeNt

7 FAMILY APGAR

Families work alone and with other families to discover ways that this simple, reliable tool for measuring satisfaction with family function can trigger growth for all family members.

GOALS

To measure levels of personal satisfaction with family relationships, using five components of family function.

To develop strategies for increasing and maintaining satisfaction with family life.

GROUP SIZE

Unlimited. Works best with family groups with kids ten years of age and older. Can also be used with individuals.

TIME FRAME

40–50 minutes.

MATERIALS

Family APGAR worksheet; newsprint; markers.

PROCESS

This process was written for family groups including parents and children but can be easily adapted to suit other groups and educational objectives. It assumes that participants have already received some orientation to family systems and healthy family relationships.

1. Begin the exercise by asking people to reflect upon the qualities of a healthy family.

   ➤ Close your eyes and think about the healthiest, happiest family you know.

      ➤ This can be a real family or a fictional family on TV, in movies, a play, or a book.

      ➤ Explore in your mind the qualities of this family: how they talk to one another, the way they listen to each other, the way they show love and affection, their style of solving problems, the kind of support they give to each family member, and the nature of the time they spend together.

➤ When you have thought of a family that you consider happy and
healthy, open your eyes.

2. Invite folks to share descriptions of the families they selected to
   represent happy, healthy clans, and write characteristics of these
   family groups on newsprint.

3. Incorporate group ideas about happy, satisfied families into a chalktalk about five components of family life that will determine the
   level of satisfaction for each family member.

   ● **Offering help when the chips are down**. Most of you want to feel
   that you could turn to your family for help if you were in trouble.
   Kids want to know that they can go to a parent, brother, or sister
   for advice about a problem at school. Parents also need each other
   and their sons and daughters to pitch in and help out during hard
   times so they feel supported and loved.

   ● **Talking over problems together.** While there are some problems
   that children cannot and should not try to solve (like their parents'
   marriage problem), there is often a sense of pride and closeness
   that comes when you can talk about problems in your family and
   help to find a solution for these problems. This gives you a sense
   of belonging and respect because your ideas and feelings count
   and are heard. It also makes it easier to cope with stress because
   you know what is happening and are not left in the dark about the
   struggles of other family members.

   ● **Supporting family members for trying new things.** Ideally, everyone in the family is encouraged to take risks and try new things
   and then is supported for doing so. If Mom wants to go back to
   college, people in the family will do whatever they can to make this
   happen: take on extra chores at home, cut back on meals out to pay
   for tuition, and give praise for the A's on her report card. If you
   are a kid and want to learn to dance, you want your parents to help
   you get signed up for a class, even if they hoped you would play
   hockey instead.

   ● **Showing affection and expressing feelings.** Everyone needs to
   know they are loved and appreciated for who they are, not just what
   they do. If you are like most people, you enjoy expressions of
   affection when they come your way: a hug or kiss, pat on the back,
   or being told you're wonderful. You probably also like to be able
   to cry if you are sad or feel angry when you are mad inside. Even
   though some feelings are hard to show because they hurt, it is

important that your family allows you to express your feelings openly and safely.

- **Enjoying time with your family.** The amount of time you have with your family is not as important as the quality of time spent with them. This is a key factor in how satisfied you will be with your family. If all your time is spent watching TV without ever talking, playing, or laughing together, you are probably going to be frustrated, unhappy, or lonely in your family circle. On the other hand, if you work at spending time together that you all enjoy—skiing, swimming, making pizza, or playing board games—you'll probably feel more content.

4. Announce that everyone will have a chance to explore their level of satisfaction with their own family in these five areas, using a tool called the **Family APGAR**. Then briefly describe the history and purpose of the APGAR in a chalktalk.

- **The APGAR was first used to measure the health of newborn babies.** Developed in 1952 by Dr. Virginia Apgar, an anesthesiologist, it became a quick and reliable method for rating a baby's health in five areas: Appearance (pink, mottled, or blue), Pulse (>100, <100, absent), Grimace (vigorous, mild, none), Activity (vigorous, lethargic, limp) and Respiratory effort (breathing and crying, gasping, not breathing.)

- In 1978, the late **Dr. Gabriel Smilkstein, a family physician, adapted the APGAR model** into a tool for measuring family support. He first used it to help medical staff plan aftercare for hospital patients using the APGAR scores of a patient's family to predict the ability of the patient's family to provide the kind of home support needed for the patient's recovery. He later expanded its use for nonmedical settings and developed tools for measuring satisfaction with other support systems, such as friends and work systems.

- **The Family APGAR is now used worldwide,** including Taiwan where it has been translated into Chinese. Many family medical centers across the United States offer the Family APGAR to all newly registered patients as part of a self-administered general medical and family history questionnaire. Family physicians, counselors, and family educators are some of the people who routinely use APGARs to help people look at their support resources.

5. Solicit questions about the **Family APGAR** and concerns about using it. Summarize common concerns in a chalktalk.

© 1997 Whole Person Associates 210 W Michigan Duluth, MN 55802   (800) 247-6789

● **Exploring any aspect of family relationships involves some risk.** Discovering how you really feel about your family interactions and listening to the perceptions of other family members can be scary. You may not be sure about how other family members will react to your perceptions or how you will react to theirs. Unexpected feelings can crop up: hurt, anger, frustration, disappointment, sadness, guilt, and anxiety as well as a possible surge of love for your family that might make you feel shy, awkward, or embarrassed.

☞ *Allow people the choice of sitting out the rest of the exercise if they do not want to take the APGAR at this time. But be sure to offer reassurance about your leadership of the process and explain the limits and ground rules for participation: no blaming, personal attacks, or put-downs allowed; keep all communication respectful and focused on opportunities for growth.*

6. Ask people to get into family groups and arrange their chairs in a circle. When everyone is settled with their family, distribute the **Family APGAR** worksheets and guide people through a reflection about levels of satisfaction with their family's function.

   ➤ For each of the five items on the worksheet, check one box that best describes your feelings about this dimension of family function: **Almost always, Some of the time,** or **Hardly ever.**

   ⁻ Check only one box for each item so you have a total of five check marks.

   ➤ Be sure to respond to all five statements.

   ☞ *Ask parents to show their children how to record their perceptions or help them go through the five statements one by one.*

7. After 2 or 3 minutes, interrupt the reflection and explain how to score the **Family APGAR** worksheet.

   ➤ Use the following scale to figure out your level of satisfaction with your family:
   ⁻ Each item marked **Almost always** = 2 points.
   ⁻ Each item marked **Some of the time** = 1 point.
   ⁻ Each item marked **Hardly ever** = 0 points.

   ➤ Add your scores for the five items to determine your total. Scores can range from 0–10.

   ☞ *Remind parents to help their children score their APGAR.*

8. When most people have scored their APGAR, explain how to interpret their scores.

⯈ A score of 0–3 = *Extremely dissatisfied* with the way your family is functioning.

⯈ A score of 4–6 = *Moderately satisfied* with family functioning with room for change or improvement.

⯈ A score of 7–10 = *Very satisfied* with the way your family is operating.

9. Once people have talked and interpreted their scores, provide guidelines for sharing responses in the family.

⯈ Starting with the oldest member of the family, go around the family circle and ask the following questions:
  ✓ What was your total satisfaction score?
  ✓ What item did you mark the highest and why?
  ✓ What item did you mark the lowest and why?

⯈ When you are the speaker, keep the focus on yourself and do not attack or blame other family members.

⯈ When you are the listener, give the speaker your full attention and support: do not interrupt, attack, blame, or judge the speaker's perceptions or comments.

⯈ You each have 3 minutes to share your responses.

⯈ The family member with a summer birthday is appointed time-keeper. If there is no summer birthday, select someone else.

10. When everyone has had a chance to share their perceptions, lead people in further reflection about areas in which they would like to maintain or increase their level of satisfaction.

⯈ As a family, discuss which area of family function you would like to work on, either to maintain at its current high level or increase to a higher level of satisfaction.

⯈ You have 3 minutes to talk it over together and decide on an area of focus.

11. Invite folks to team up with another family and brainstorm strategies for increasing or maintaining satisfaction on their chosen area of family function.

⯈ Circulate around the room and find another family who wants to work on the same area of family function that you do.

  ☞ *Facilitate the process by designating five areas of the room where families can gather to meet people interested in a particular family function.*

12. When each family has joined with another family to create a team, give each team a sheet of newsprint and a marker, and explain how they can pool their resources to create new strategies for increasing family member's satisfaction with their area of specialty.

> You have just become a panel of experts in family education, and your challenge is to generate a list of creative ideas and strategies for building or maintaining family satisfaction in your selected area of family life.

> You have 4 minutes to brainstorm a list of ideas and strategies, and then choose three of your best ideas as recommendations to share with the large group.

> The oldest teenager in your family team is appointed recorder and writes all the ideas on a newsprint. If there is not a teenager in the group, select another family member.

> Humorous, playful ideas are encouraged. Try to have fun with this part.

☞ *Remind people when time is half up, and again when there is 1 minute left.*

13. Interrupt the discussions and invite each team in turn to share their favorite three recommendations with the large group.

☞ *Affirm each team for their creative ideas.*

14. Summarize ideas about the value of teamwork, support, and satisfaction in a final chalktalk, incorporating tips on how to use the APGAR acronym as a guide for building a healthy and happy family system.

● **Teamwork is a hallmark of supportive family systems.** When family members pool resources and put their heads together to solve a problem, the synergy that develops is like a ripple of support that flows throughout the family. The burden of each family member may grow lighter while feelings of commitment and closeness between family members will probably increase. This is likely to make people in the family feel supported which, in turn, leads to greater satisfaction with family life.

● **Building family support is hard work but satisfying in the long run.** Tending to family relationships takes time and patience. The rewards are not always apparent, and you may wonder, "Why bother?" But once family members begin to grow and thrive in the supportive environment you have created, and you begin to experience an increase in your own sense of well-being, you'll be glad you invested time and energy into developing and maintaining a system that nurtures all of its members, including you.

● **Use your APGAR as a guide for building family support.**

A = Adaptation. Change is stressful. Help people when they need it.

P = Partnership. Work together to make decisions and solve problems.

G = Growth. Support family members in their efforts to change and grow.

A = Affection. Show love and affection. Encourage healthy expression of feelings.

R = Resolve. Make a commitment to spend quality time with your family.

VARIATIONS

▦ Use with couples only or with individual adults who want to explore their satisfaction with their family support system. People who live alone should consider as family those with whom they have the strongest emotional ties.

▦ Change into a **Friends APGAR** by substituting the word friends for family and score in the same way.

▦ The **Work APGAR** is described in *Structured Exercises in Wellness Promotion, Volume 5* (Duluth, Minnesota: Whole Person Associates, 1995).

Contributed by the late Gabriel Smilkstein, M.D.

FAMILY APGAR

Family is the individual(s) with whom you usually live. If you live alone, consider as family those with whom you now have the strongest emotional ties.

For each of the five items, check one box that best describes your response. Please respond to all five items. Use the **Comments** space to give additional information or to describe the way the question applies to your family.

	Almost always	Some of the time	Hardly ever
I am satisfied that I can turn to my family for help when something is troubling me.	❏	❏	❏
Comments:			
I am satisfied with the way my family talks over things with me and shares problems with me.	❏	❏	❏
Comments:			
I am satisfied that my family accepts and supports my wishes to take on new activities or directions.	❏	❏	❏
Comments:			
I am satisfied with the way my family expresses affection and responds to my emotions, such as anger, sorrow, or love.	❏	❏	❏
Comments:			
I am satisfied with the way my family and I share time together.	❏	❏	❏
Comments:			

8 HEALTHY FAMILY CONTINUUM

This simple subjective measurement of family health enables people to see whether they are repeating unhealthy childhood family patterns in their present family and, if so, to decide what they want to do about it.

GOALS

To deepen personal awareness of the role family of origin played in shaping current family relationships.

To develop goals and strategies for changing one dimension of family health.

GROUP SIZE

Unlimited. Works well with individuals.

TIME FRAME

60–90 minutes.

MATERIALS NEEDED

Healthy Family Continuum worksheet; newsprint; marker; masking tape; blank name tags and 3" x 5" cards for all participants.

PROCESS

1. Begin with an icebreaker based on one of the traits of healthy families—respect for differences. Hand out name tags and give directions for introductions. (3–5 minutes)

   ➤ On your name tag, write your first name and one way you think you are different from other people.

   ➤ Introduce yourself by stating your first name and telling what is unique or different about you.

      Some people will invariably be clowns and think of funny things. Use this time as an opportunity to create a lighthearted, accepting group atmosphere. Remember to include yourself in the process and share something unique about yourself.

2. After introductions, point out that respect for differences is one trait of healthy families that you hope participants will experience during the time you have together. Outline the session content and process,

then review other ground rules (confidentiality, voluntary participation, etc.).

3. Give a brief chalktalk on the healthy family continuum.

   ● **Family health can be viewed on a continuum,** with very stressful or troubled relationships at one end and very healthy or satisfying relationships at the other. Most families fall somewhere between these extremes. Location on the continuum changes (for better or worse) with different circumstances (when Grandma lay dying, Mom was depressed, your family couldn't talk about problems, or when Mom and Dad went to a marriage encounter).

   ● **There are usually things you can do to move toward health** or to maintain healthy relationships in your family. Communicating feelings clearly and respectfully, solving problems, changing family rules—many things can enhance family functioning and health.

   ● **Creating healthy family relationships is a lifelong process.** Because people change, you are constantly challenged to adjust. Perhaps your family was very close and happy during your children's school years—but then your kids grew up, married, and moved away from home, and you and your spouse were faced with getting to know each other all over again. Your place on the continuum of health may have changed depending on how you responded to these changes.

4. Remind people about the importance of their family of origin in shaping their patterns of relating in their current family.

   ● **Your family of origin is your first relationship school.** It is where you first learned about families—how they connect, communicate, show love, solve problems, and achieve goals. Kids learn from watching their parents, grandparents, foster parents, and other important adults interact with each other, with children, and with other people. This is a powerful education, one we receive at a time when we are dependent, vulnerable, and impressionable.

   ● **Early family relationships are your template or blueprint** for relationships. You may not follow exact patterns of your family, but you probably copied at least some of the habits of your ancestors—your Dad's stoicism at times of grief and loss, your Mother's caretaking, your family's style of joking about serious feelings.

   ● **Knowing your family blueprint can help you.** Self-awareness can enhance your ability to make conscious choices about your behavior—to recognize what you are doing, why you are doing it, and how you can change it.

5. Invite participants to explore the health of their family of origin at different points of time using a human continuum model. (6–8 minutes)

> *Caution people to refrain from making judgments about themselves or others because of their position on the continuum. Remind people that families move from unhealthy to healthy points at various times under different circumstances. Also remind people about confidentiality.*

> Stand up and pretend there is an imaginary line along the wall representing a continuum of health. The left end represents highly stressed or troubled family relationships, and the right end represents healthy, satisfying relationships.

> Position yourself at the point on the continuum which represents how healthy your family of origin was *when you were six years old.*

>> Feel free to move around or change positions until it feels right to you.

> When everyone is in their final place on the continuum, turn to the person next to you and share why you placed yourself at this spot on the continuum.

>> What was going on in your family when you were six that made you place yourself at this particular point?

6. After a few minutes of sharing, ask participants to explore the health of their childhood family at other times in their life, guiding people through each step of the process.

> Now move to the spot that represents your family of origin's health *when you were twelve years old.*

> Tell the person next to you why you choose this spot.

>> If you changed your position on the continuum, describe factors you think caused this change in your family health.

>> If you stayed in the same spot, tell why or how your family maintained its former state of health.

> Now move to the spot on the continuum that represents your family's health *when you were 18 years old.*

>> Tell the person next to you what caused your family's health to change or stay the same at this time in your life.

7. Ask everyone to be seated and invite folks to share examples of things that caused their family's health to decline. List health-diminishing events or variables on newsprint.

☞ *The list might look like this: divorce, siblings leaving home, illness/ death, remarriage, alcohol and drug abuse, money problems, violence, etc.*

8. After you have identified health-diminishing variables, ask participants to share examples of factors that caused their family's health to improve. List these health-promoting variables on newsprint.

☞ *Your list might include religious faith, pulling together in a crisis, kids maturing, family counseling, chemical dependency treatment, education, money, etc.*

9. Summarize factors having a positive influence on family health, weaving ideas into a chalktalk on eight qualities of healthy family systems.

● **Commitment.** When you make your family a priority in your life, you put quality time and energy into building the kind of relationships you can rely on. This means working through problems with care and respect.

● **Connection.** When you feel connected in your family, you feel like you belong. You also feel like you contribute something to the family and are an important part of its function and purpose. You have a sense of belonging to a large social network or community as well. This is in contrast to the isolation and alienation that can exist in overstressed families.

● **Communication.** Ideally, your family is a place where you can be open and honest about what you feel and think. Secrecy and denial do not exist: there is nothing you cannot talk about.

● **Safety**. Safety means being cared for physically and psychologically. You can be yourself and trust that you will not be abandoned. You can trust other family members to be consistent, reasonable, and reliable. This means no violence, no physical, verbal, emotional, or sexual abuse.

● **Respect**. When your family is nurturing, you are accepted and appreciated for who you are, not for what others want you to be. It is OK to be different; your uniqueness is acknowledged and valued.

● **Boundaries.** A boundary is a clear, invisible circle of space around you and everyone in your family, drawing a line between you and other family members. When boundaries are respected, you have some control over when and how other people enter your physical and emotional space, so you do not feel invaded and your privacy is honored.

Flexible rules. Rules work best when they are not rigid or used to enforce unnatural stability in the family. Because people and circumstance change, rules need to be flexible, used as guidelines for negotiation and problem solving. This gives the freedom necessary for adjusting to change.

Change. Family health depends not so much on what happens in your family but on how your family responds to change. When your family is troubled, you will probably fight change because it is too threatening; when your family is healthy, you expect change as a fact of life and use it as an opportunity for adjusting family relationships to fit changing circumstances.

10. Distribute the **Healthy Family Continuum** worksheets and guide people in exploring the extent to which these eight qualities of family health were present in their *family of origin* and *in their current adult/family relationships*. Review the eight qualities as needed. (3–5 minutes)

   ➤ On each of the eight dimensions of family health, circle the number that best represents the extent to which this trait was present in your **family of origin**.

   ➤ Base your rating on the time when you were *between the ages of three and seven* years old, using specific incidents from this period of time as a guide for making your evaluation.

   ➤ 1 = the lowest rating, indicating a relative absence of this trait.

   ➤ 10 = the highest rating, indicating a very strong presence of this trait.

   ➤ Now go back to the beginning of the scale and place a star beside the point on the continuum that best describes the degree to which these eight healthy traits are present in your **current family or adult relationships.**

   ➤ Be as honest as you can, using recent situations and incidents to decide on a rating based on your actions, not your feelings or beliefs.

11. Invite people to look at each continuum again, this time considering which areas of family health they would like to strengthen in the future.

> Draw an arrow at the place on the scale **where you would like to be** in your relationships.

>> Try to set a realistic, achievable goal for the near future, perhaps three months from now.

>>> *Caution people to set realistic goals so they don't end up discouraged or give up on efforts to change.*

> Now look over the eight factors again and choose one as a top priority for change over the next three months.

12. Ask people to share the area of family health they chose to work on forming small groups based on these chosen interests. Designate an area of the room where each group can gather and give each group two blank sheets of newsprint and a marker. Then outline instructions for brainstorming steps toward family health.

> Ask someone to volunteer as group recorder to write down the group's ideas on newsprint.

> In 3 minutes brainstorm as many ideas as you can for moving your family toward health in your chosen area of family function.

13. When 2–3 minutes have passed, interrupt group discussions and give additional instructions for selecting ideas they want to share with other participants. (5–6 minutes)

> The person with the largest shoe size will act as a footprint model.

>> Stand on the other blank newsprint while another group member traces the outline of your shoe or footprint three times on paper so you have a total of three footprints on newsprint.

> As a group, look over your first list of ideas and select three you want to recommend as steps for change on this dimension of family health.

>> Write one step for change inside each of the three footprints on your newsprint.

14. Invite reporters to come to the front of the room one at a time, hang their steps for change on a wall or blackboard, and give a short presentation on these recommendations.

15. When group presentations are finished, ask people to return to their seats for a final reflection on personal steps for change.

> Now consider the steps you personally want to take towards health in your family.

© 1997 Whole Person Associates 210 W Michigan Duluth, MN 55802   (800) 247-6789

➤ On the right side of your **Healthy Family Continuum** worksheet, describe the steps you will take to move along the healthy family continuum toward your goal.

16. When everyone has had time to reflect on personal goals for change, invite folks to share learnings and goals with another person. (4–5 minutes)

➤ Pair up with someone you do not know well. Share what you have learned today and what steps you will take to move to your healthy family goals.

17. Invite participants to share what they learned in the workshop and then lead participants in an enthusiastic affirmation exercise. Hand out blank 3" x 5" cards and give directions.

➤ Write your name on your card and one of the strengths you bring to your family.

18. Collect all cards and read them aloud one at a time. Encourage the group to get involved in the affirmation process with standing ovations.

➤ When you hear your name and your strength read aloud, stand up and take a bow while everyone else gives you a standing ovation for the unique quality you bring to your family.

➤ This is the time to get rowdy—yell, cheer, whistle, clap, stamp your feet in approval for the person who is standing in the limelight.

VARIATION

For a quick assessment and planning process, use the chalktalk introduction to eight healthy family traits followed by individual reflection, planning, and sharing of ideas for change using the **Healthy Family Continuum** worksheets. Drop the family of origin continuum in *Steps 5* and *6,* the group brainstorming and presentations in *Steps 12–14,* and the affirmation process in *Steps 17* and *18.*

Adapted from the work of Stephanie Covington and Liana Beckett, using a model presented in their book Leaving the Enchanted Forest: The Path from Relationship Addiction to Intimacy *(San Francisco: Harper & Row, 1988).*

HEALTHY FAMILY CONTINUUM

Circle the number on the continuum that best represents the extent to which this trait was present in your **family of origin.** (1 = lowest, 10 = highest)

Place a **star** by the number on the continuum that represents your **current family or adult relationships.**

Draw an **arrow** at the place **where you would like to be in your relationships.** Determine steps you can take toward change.

Traits   **My steps for change**

Commitment

1   2   3   4   5   6   7   8   9   10

Connection

1   2   3   4   5   6   7   8   9   10

Communication

1   2   3   4   5   6   7   8   9   10

Safety

1   2   3   4   5   6   7   8   9   10

Respect

1   2   3   4   5   6   7   8   9   10

Boundaries

1   2   3   4   5   6   7   8   9   10

Flexible rules

1   2   3   4   5   6   7   8   9   10

Change

1   2   3   4   5   6   7   8   9   10

9 FAMILY LIFE CYCLE

This engaging, multifaceted exercise uses creative arts, family sculpture, small group sharing, and personal reflection to make learning about the family life cycle fun as well as educational.

GOALS

To learn about the family life cycle and the challenges of each stage.

To identify personal stages of family development and explore progress in completing family tasks.

GROUP SIZE

Unlimited. Works best with multiple family groups but can also be done with groups of individuals.

TIME FRAME

60–90 minutes.

MATERIALS NEEDED

Newsprint (two sheets) and a variety of colored markers for each small group; masking tape; nine posters or signs labeled with each stage of the family life cycle, hung at designated locations around the room prior to the session; **Family Life Cycle** worksheet.

PROCESS

1. Introduce the family life cycle as a natural process that has been observed for centuries.

   - **All civilizations have recognized the family life cycle.** The sequential stages of life from birth to death have been recorded in history, religion, cultural rituals, novels, drama, and art since earliest time. The birth of a child, the launching of a young adult, the decline and death of an elder family member—all are normal life changes, routinely dealt with, celebrated, mourned, marked, and remembered by families around the world.

   - **Theories of family life cycle were developed only recently.** In the first half of the twentieth century, the focus was on individual development, especially the normal stages of child development, à la Drs. Spock, Erickson, and Gesell.

In their 1980 book, *Family Life Cycle: A Framework for Family Therapy*, social workers Elizabeth Carter and Monica McGoldrick identified six normal stages of family life (single adult, couple, family with young children, family with adolescents, family with adult children, and family in later life) and three special types of families (divorced with coparent, single parent with no coparent, and stepfamilies).

2. Point out the nine family stages and structures posted on signs around the room, reading each stage sign aloud in sequential order. Invite families to form discussion groups with other families who are in their same stage of the family life cycle.

   ➤ Which stage is your family in now?

       ☞ *Many families will be in more than one stage of development at a time. Ask families to choose one stage to focus on during this exercise.*

   ➤ Stand up and move to the signpost location that you think represents your current stage in the family life cycle or the stage you want to focus on during this exercise.

   ➤ Introduce yourself to other families gathered at this developmental signpost and then find a place to sit down together.

       ➤ If your group is larger than twelve people, divide into smaller groups (six to twelve people). It's OK to split up your family.

3. When everyone has joined an appropriate life cycle group, distribute newsprint and markers to each group. Give instructions for creating a group mural depicting their stage of the family life cycle.

   ➤ Create a drawing or mural that represents the issues, frustrations, challenges, and joys of this family life stage.

       ➤ Work cooperatively as a group to decide what to include on your mural, allowing everyone, including children, the opportunity to add pictures, symbols, and words.

       ➤ There is no right way to do this. Be creative and illustrate your mural anyway you want.

       ➤ You have 10 minutes to create your family life cycle mural.

   ➤ The person who is closest to age twenty-five in your group is appointed curator and will present your final artwork to the large group.

4. After 10 minutes, announce that it is time to display team artwork in

a gallery which will show all the developmental stages of family life. Ask team curators to hang pictures in developmental sequence on a wall or blackboard, then present their teams mural to the large group.

> Briefly explain your picture, summarizing key issues identified by your group for this stage of family life.

5. Thank curators and family teams for creative life cycle stories and pictures and ask everyone to be seated. Hand out the **Family Life Cycle** worksheets. Invite everyone to follow along on their worksheet as you present family life cycle stages using family sculpture for demonstration. Pause after each stage and allow time for participants to reflect on their personal progress through this stage.

   Give all children a worksheet. Older children (ten years and up) can do their own, younger children can work with parents, listen quietly, and volunteer for the family sculpture demonstration.

   Young adult. Your task is to begin adult-to-adult relationships with your parents, develop close friends, and establish yourself in work.

   Sculpt this stage by asking a volunteer to come up alone, pick two people to be his parents and two people to be his friends. Have the young adult stand slightly apart from his parents with his friends, yet smiling at his parents.

   > Check the box that best describes your progress in moving through this stage (completed it, in progress, or not done). Write other reflections about this stage in the space to the right on each task.

   Couples. Your task is to commit yourself to teamwork and realign yourself with family and friends to include your partner.

   Ask a young man to recruit a partner and then invite them to come to the front of the room. The couple stands close together while you describe the challenges of a newly formed couple. Add two parents to one side, both holding the hand of their child, to demonstrate visually the step from the family of origin into the new family. Ask what they might be saying to their child as he is about to marry. Show the push and pull as they hold on and let go with their adult child and open up to a new in-law.

   > Record reflections about your movement through this stage of life on your worksheet.

   Family with a young child. Now you must take on parenting and leadership roles, making room for your children's needs in your relationship. This involves actively negotiating grandparents' roles and saving some time for being a couple.

> *Add a small child, asking the audience where the child would be as a newborn (alternating between Mom's and Dad's arms, with Mom and Dad close) and where the child would be on the first day of school (have parents put their outer arms on the child, who stands a bit in front of them, and their inner hands holding onto each other). Have the grandparents standing together, nearby.*

> Note your progress through this stage on your worksheet.

● **Family with adolescent.** Parents need to work more cooperatively and gradually share more decision-making with teenagers. You will need to make room for your teen to get more involved outside the family and start to focus more on yourselves, your careers, marriage, and aging parents and less on your teenager.

> *Have the young child sit down. Bring a teen to the front of the room. After noting their different tastes in music, dress, etc., have the teen face away from the parents, say things like, "Can I borrow the car tonight . . . When's dinner?" The teenager should be farther from the parents than the younger child was. Have grandparents and parents a bit closer together than in earlier stages.*

> Record your progress in handling the challenges of raising a teenager and write reflections about this stage in the margin.

● **Family with adult children.** Your adult children now become more involved away from the family than within it, developing their own friendships and economic support. Adult relationships develop between parents and grown children, and partners renew their commitment to one another.

> *Declare the teen now a young adult child with the challenge to earn a living and to develop an adult relationship with their parents. Have the young adult stand beside and apart from parents, as equals. Parents now move closer still to grandparents. State that one grandparent dies and the other reaches to their daughter or son for support.*

> Mark the box that describes your progress in completing this stage and add other reflections about this stage.

● **Family in later life.** Your children are more involved outside of the family than in it. Adult relationships develop between parents and grown children. Your family expands to include in-laws and grandchildren, and you renew romance and commitments with your partner or, if your partner is deceased, begin to explore new relationships.

> *Have adult children stand a little farther apart with a new partner of their own and a new child. Surviving adult finds new partner, who comes to stand next to them, holding hands or standing close.*

> If you are in this stage, record your reflections about how it's going so far by marking the appropriate boxes and adding notes relevant to your experience.

6. Introduce the concept of special family stages, including divorce, single parenting, and stepfamilies, emphasizing what it takes for the family to stay healthy through these changes.

   Divorced coparents. The task here is to end the spousal agreement but retain coparenting. The child keeps ties to each parent, and each parent is in charge in their own household.

   > *Take the same two adults you began with and have them stand apart, declaring them divorced. Have the ten-year-old child go back and forth between them and, occasionally, to the grandparents.*

   > If you are a divorced coparent, how is it going? Write notes to yourself on your worksheet using the boxes as a guide.

   Single parent with no coparent. In this situation, you need to stay in charge and rely heavily on consultants like friends and extended family. You need at least one close adult friend, and adult household members should be in the role of advisor or helper, not coparent.

   > *Have one parent leave the area to show a single parent with no coparent, with the child moving closer to that one parent.*

   > If you are a single parent without a coparent, mark the boxes that represent your progress in completing tasks of this stage.

   Stepfamilies. Now you must commit to a new partnership and develop a coparenting agreement. Your child has access to both parents, to stepparents, and to grandparents. Adults cooperatively take charge of all children in the household.

   > *Have the single parent remarry with the new spouse bringing a child from a former marriage, new grandparents, and a new baby between them.*

➤ If you are remarried, check the boxes of tasks mastered and record tasks yet to be completed.

7. Close with the comment: "So who is the family? . . . All of them! No matter the size or stage of your family, you must *be* a family and be ready to change.

8. Acknowledge the difficulty of family transitions in a brief chalktalk.

   ● **Change is difficult for all families.** You might struggle more with one stage than another, but over the long haul, the difficulty of adjusting to each new stage of life is balanced out: all are challenging!

   ● **Every family has strengths.** Your family has its own toolbox or treasure chest, filled with unique tricks for getting through difficult stages. Everyone has something that works, a skill or strategy that has helped your family grow into new, healthy ways of relating.

9. Ask participants to rejoin their family life stage group, share success stories, and extract helpful learning that can be passed on to other participants. Give each group another newsprint and marker and provide guidelines for sharing. (10 minutes)

   ➤ Spend the next 6–8 minutes sharing success stories, anecdotes, or memories of what has helped your family move through previous developmental stages and cope effectively with the challenges of your current stage.

   ➤ Select a reporter to take notes on a blank sheet of paper, saving the newsprint for your team's final words of wisdom, which each group will share later with the large group.

   ➤ After you have developed a list of past and present success stories, review your list and decide as a group what important learning or skills you want to pass on or recommend to other participants.

     ➤ In 4 minutes, select three of the most important or helpful things you've learned about where you are now and three things you've learned from where you have been that you'd like to share with other participants.

     ➤ Reporters transfer these six final words of wisdom about past and present learning to the newsprint.

10. Ask reporters to take turns coming to the front of the room to share their family team's wisdom. Conclude by complimenting everyone present on their participation as well as their strengths.

VARIATIONS

- For a shorter program, drop the mural activity in *Steps 3* and *4* using brief group discussions and brainstorming instead.

- *Steps 5* and *6* could be modified by leaving out the family sculpture demonstrations. Use a simple chalktalk, incorporating participants' examples of family stories to enliven the discussion.

This exercise was contributed by Virginia Morgan Scott, who credits Elizabeth A. Carter and Monica McGoldrick for the original family life cycle model.

FAMILY LIFE CYCLE

	completed	in progress	not done	Reflections

Young adult

	completed	in progress	not done
Develop adult-to-adult relationship with parents	❏	❏	❏
Develop friendships with other young adults	❏	❏	❏
Establish career plans or goals	❏	❏	❏

Couple

Develop ability to work as a team	❏	❏	❏
Carve out time to be alone as a couple	❏	❏	❏
Include partner/relationship with family, friends	❏	❏	❏

Family with young children

Develop parenting roles	❏	❏	❏
Establish parenting authority with grandparents	❏	❏	❏
Maintain some couple time apart from children	❏	❏	❏

Family with adolescents

Cooperate with coparent	❏	❏	❏
Develop more shared decision-making with teens	❏	❏	❏
Refocus on adult/parent interests	❏	❏	❏

Family with adult children

Develop involvement/interests outside family	❏	❏	❏
Expand family to include adult child's new friends and interests	❏	❏	❏
Renew communication with adult partner	❏	❏	❏

Family in later life

Expand involvement outside family	❏	❏	❏
Expand family membership (grandchildren)	❏	❏	❏
Renew romance with adult partner	❏	❏	❏

Divorced with coparent

End spousal agreement with ex-spouse	❏	❏	❏
Retain coparenting agreement with ex-spouse	❏	❏	❏
Maintain/support children's ties to both parents	❏	❏	❏

Single parent with no coparent

Stay in charge as a parent	❏	❏	❏
Rely on trustworthy adults for consultation/support	❏	❏	❏
Develop and maintain adult friendships and a social life	❏	❏	❏

Stepfamilies

Develop relationship with new partner	❏	❏	❏
Develop coparenting agreement with new partner	❏	❏	❏
Help children have access to all relatives, including grandparents	❏	❏	❏

10 HOLISTIC HAND-ME-DOWNS

This healing process helps people recognize that, while they may not have received everything they needed from their parents, they probably received nurturing in some areas, allowing them to develop unique strengths and gifts.

GOALS

To identify and appreciate unique childhood gifts received from an individual's family of origin: emotional, mental, physical, relational, and spiritual nurturing.

GROUP SIZE

Unlimited.

TIME FRAME

45–50 minutes.

MATERIALS NEEDED

Five dolls, preferably multicultural dolls and, for a humorous touch, one Barbie or Ken doll; **Holistic Hand-Me-Downs** worksheet; newsprint; markers; masking tape.

PROCESS

1. Begin by asking participants to reflect on the quality of nurturing received in their family of origin.

    ✔ How many of you would say you received *ideal, holistic* nurturing on all levels of development: emotional, mental, physical, relational, and spiritual?

    ☞ *List the five areas on newsprint for later reference. Ask people to raise their hands to indicate a yes response to the question. Probably only a few will raise their hands; acknowledge the good fortune of those who do. If a large number of people respond affirmatively, note this as exceptional and cause for celebration.*

2. Integrate participant responses into a brief chalktalk about ideal, holistic nurturing.

● **Ideally, we would all receive holistic nurturing as children.** In a perfect world, your family of origin would carefully nurture all aspects of your development—emotional, mental, physical, relational, and spiritual—so you would have a better chance of growing into a healthy, happy, loving, productive adult.

● **The world is imperfect and so are families.** Most new parents want the best for their babies but other realties interfere with ideal parenting. Economic (having to work two jobs or a night shift), social (isolation, racism), and psychological (insecurity, low self-esteem) conditions all affect the quality and quantity of nurturing parents can give children.

3. Divide participants into five small groups (one for each area of development: physical, mental, emotional, relational, and spiritual) by asking people to number off by area of development. Assign a spot in the room where each group can gather.

4. When all five groups are settled, give each group a doll, newsprint, and a marker, and explain that a short group fantasy will be used as a method of drawing out memories and ideas associated with ideal nurturing. (5–10 minutes)

   ➤ Imagine that you are all new parents of this baby and that you are about to plan ways of providing ideal nurturing for your baby in your assigned area of development. (emotional, mental, physical, relational, or spiritual)

   ➤ Beginning with the oldest grandparent or parent in the group, each person in turns holds the baby for 1 minute and talks about what they will do to nurture it in the area assigned to your group.

   ➤ After 1 minute, the baby is handed to the next person, who shares a different idea for nurturing your baby on this dimension, and so forth around the group, until everyone in the group has held the baby and shared a unique idea for its development.

   ➤ Ask the youngest member of your group to be the **group reporter.** Write each idea for nurturing your baby on your newsprint and be ready to share these ideas with the large group.

5. When everyone has had the opportunity to share nurturing ideas with their group, interrupt discussions and call on group reporters one at a time to present group strategies for ideal nurturing.

   ☞ *Ask reporters to bring their newsprint to the front of the room so you can hang it on a wall or blackboard while they briefly explain their ideas to the audience.*

6. After all five groups have presented their ideas for nurturing, invite participants to look over the entire collection of ideas for holistic family nurturing and reflect on the kind of nurturing they received in their own family of origin.

7. Distribute the**Holistic Hand-Me-Downs**worksheets, and lead people in further reflection about the heirlooms they received from their family of origin.

> Close your eyes, take a deep breath, release tension by exhaling slowly and allowing yourself to relax. Now focus on the type of nurturing you received in your own family, the actions, events, or attitudes which nourished your emotional, mental, physical, relational, and spiritual development.

> What were some of the ways you were nurtured *emotionally?* (Were you allowed to cry and express other emotions, told you were loved and lovable?)

>> Write the ways you were nurtured emotionally in the space for emotional hand-me-downs on your worksheet.

>> If you bump into bad memories, simply acknowledge them and move on, continuing to look for positive gifts, experiences, or events that helped you to grow and become the unique, wonderful person you are now.

> How were you nourished *mentally?* (Were you challenged to think for yourself, solve problems and puzzles, read?)

>> Write examples of mental nourishment you received from your family.

> What kinds of *physical* nurturing did you receive? (Did your parents feed you healthy food, encourage exercise and movement, teach you to love and respect your body?)

>> Write examples of physical nourishment you received as a child.

> In what way did your family nurture your *relationships* as a child? (Did they encourage you to make new friends, join social groups like scouts, play team sports, or work out conflicts with your pals?)

>> Write examples of ways your family nurtured your childhood relationships.

> How was your *spirituality* nourished in your family? (Did you practice a specific religion, pray together with your family, read the Bible or other books exploring spiritual values and beliefs?)

➤ Write examples of the kind of spiritual nurturing you received in your family.

8. When everyone has had a chance to reflect on nurturing childhood experiences, invite people to share their gifts with a neighbor.

➤ Pair up with someone you do not know well and take turns sharing whatever you wish about holistic hand-me-downs you received from your family.

➤ Each of you has 3 minutes to share your endowment.

9. After about 8 minutes, reconvene the group and invite participants to share discoveries with the large group.

✔ What new discoveries did you make about your family inheritance?

✔ Were there any surprises in your dowry?

10. Conclude with a chalktalk about the importance of identifying and celebrating gifts received from your family of origin.

● **Just as it is important to grieve your losses, it's important to celebrate your gifts.** If your childhood has been troubled or traumatic, it's easy to overlook the good things you received from your family. In some circumstances, it's hard to find anything positive in your family. But you probably received some nurturing or you wouldn't be here or be the interesting person you have become. At the most basic level, you received life and an opportunity to grow and survive. This gift is *always* cause for celebration.

VARIATION

▢ If you are working with an ongoing group, you could ask people to bring in five objects from home which are symbolic of emotional, mental, physical, relational, and spiritual nurturing received from their family of origin. Ask them to share a story about each object with the group.

HOLISTIC HAND-ME-DOWNS

Emotional:

Mental:

Physical:

Relational:

Spiritual:

11 LIVING IN STEP: FANTASY AND REALITY

These exercises provide a safe, respectful process for stepfamily members to explore fantasies and realities of living in a stepfamily, discover what they have in common with other stepfamilies, and lay the groundwork for healthy stepfamily development.

GOALS

To explore fantasies and realities of stepfamily life and share experiences with other stepfamily members.

To identify feelings about stepfamily experiences, find a voice to express those feelings, and develop an understanding of other family members' feelings.

To normalize the often intense and sometimes painful feelings of early stepfamily life.

GROUP SIZE

Unlimited.

TIME FRAME

90 minutes–4 hours.

MATERIALS NEEDED

Newsprint; marker; **Stepfamily Perspectives** worksheet.

PROCESS

☞ *The shorter time frame is most appropriate for educational contexts and facilitators who are not clinically trained. With groups of stepfamilies experiencing significant difficulty, the longer workshop format is more desirable and therapeutic, as long as the leader is prepared to handle the group and family dynamics.*

This exercise was written for stepfamily groups including children but can be adapted easily for adults-only groups.

Many stepfamily members have significant shame about their stepfamily fantasies. If their family of origin was shaming about expressing personal wants or needs, it can be especially difficult to disclose fantasies or let go of them. Keep this in mind throughout the session, and make sure the group process stays respectful and accepting.

1. Begin with a short introductory exercise to help people get acquainted and comfortable in the group. Allow 5–10 minutes for this process.

   > One person in each family please stand up, introduce everyone in your family, tell who is related to whom, and tell how long you have been together.

2. When introductions are completed, discuss ground rules about confidentiality, respect, and acceptance of all participants. Then lead participants in another icebreaker that will allow people to share positive and negative stepfamily experiences with other participants. Spend 5–10 minutes on this icebreaker.

   > Pair up with someone you do not know well—kids can pair with other kids if you choose—and find a place to sit down together.

   > Share one thing that is going well for you in your stepfamily. Then tell briefly about one hard or difficult thing for you to handle.

     > Share at the level you feel comfortable.

     > You each have 2–4 minutes to share so you will have time for just a few headlines.

3. Reconvene the group and solicit a few examples of good and bad experiences. Use the responses as a bridge to your chalktalk on common stepfamily fantasies.

   ● Today we're going to talk about the fantasies we bring to our stepfamily relationships and the sometimes surprising and painful realities that stepfamilies normally encounter. Learning what's normal—and being able to talk about it—can make a huge difference in enhancing stepfamily development.

   ● **Fantasies are normal in all new relationships.** We all have fantasies about what a new relationship is going to be like—exciting, fun, peaceful, or whatever we imagine it to be. We all create images about new relationships, in part because we need to know what is going to happen and because we want things to go well. Fantasies are like dreaming about something you want or need.

   ● **In stepfamilies, there are particular kinds of fantasies** because of the way stepfamilies come together (from previous families separated by divorce or death and brought together by remarriage of adults). Biological parents, stepparents, and children all have fantasies, which are normal for new stepfamily relationships.

   ● **For biological parents,** the following fantasies are common:

     ○ **I love my son/daughter, so of course my partner will love**

her/him in the same way I do. Of course biological parents would want new partners to love their biological children in the same way they do. It's a joy to share your love and pride for your children with someone else. Unfortunately, normal stepfamily dynamics make this almost impossible.

○ **If I love my new partner, obviously my kids will too.** You love your new partner so much, it's hard to imagine that your kids would not feel the same way. It can be terribly disappointing when it doesn't work out that way.

○ **If my new partner doesn't love my kids, my partner must not love me.** Because biological parents are so strongly connected to their children, it's hard not to feel rejected or hurt when your new partner doesn't feel as attached as you do.

○ **This new family will heal the hurts and disappointments of my previous family.** If you hope for things like peace, easy affection, and clear rules, early stepfamily life can be very frustrating.

○ **This new marriage will heal hurts remaining from my family of origin.** If you came from a family of origin where there were chronic disappointments or inadequate caretaking, then you have an extra need to hope for your new marriage to heal these hurts—and it's extra painful when it doesn't.

● **For stepparents,** the following fantasies are common:

○ **I love my new partner, so of course I'll love his/her kids.** You assume that your feelings will come easily or automatically as part of your love for your partner, and it's easy to feel guilty when it doesn't work this way.

○ **I will provide what the previous parent did not—and won't the children be grateful!** I can fill some of the gaps left by the previous parent—for affection, discipline, etc. Since there is an obvious need for these things, my efforts will be appreciated and welcomed. It can be stunning when children reject a stepparent's efforts, as they often do.

○ **It will be easier for us with two adults in the family.** This hope is shared by both stepparents and biological parents. It is true that in some ways having two adults will make things easier, but in other ways it will not, due to the complexity of stepfamily development.

● **Children's fantasies are often very different from adults.** Their coping skills and problem-solving experience are more limited.

They are developmentally self-absorbed and see the world in concrete terms. For children in stepfamilies, the following fantasies are common:

If I can be indifferent or nasty enough, I can get rid of this intruder. It is tough for adults to understand just how difficult it is for kids to have an adult in their life whom they didn't choose. While some children may fantasize about having lots of fun with their new stepparent, many hope that if they keep their distance or are hostile, their stepparent will leave the family. Grown-ups experience this resistance of kids as mean and nasty.

Having new kids in the family will be fun. Biological children are not aware of how intruded upon they may feel or how awkward it is for new stepsiblings to be in somebody else's house and live under their rules. Stepsiblings feel like they are in a strange place where little is familiar to them.

4. Invite participants to comment on these fantasies by asking these questions:

✔ Are any of these fantasies familiar to you?

✔ Do you have any others that aren't on this list?

5. Solicit a few examples and use them as a segue to a chalktalk about the realities of living in a stepfamily.

Now that we have talked about typical fantasies, **it is time to look at realities.** Letting go of your fantasies can be painful. But working with and talking respectfully about the realities of stepfamily life will give your family its best chance for successful development. Let's look briefly at some normal stepfamily dynamics. As you listen, consider how these concepts apply to your stepfamily situation.

In a stepfamily there are *stuck insiders* and *stuck outsiders*. This is different from other families, which (when working well) have insider and outsider roles that rotate from person to person depending on circumstances. For example, sometimes Mom and Dad will be alone, and kids will be left out. At other times, Dad and children will play together, and Mom is left out.

In stepfamilies, biological parents are *stuck insiders* who are more connected to their biological kids or ex-spouse, while stepparents are *stuck outsiders* who do not share the relationship history of biological parents and children. The older biological relationship is stronger, especially in the early years.

When biological parent, biological child, and stepparent are in a room together, often one person will be left out, especially in early stepfamily life. Who will be left out? Usually it's the stepparent, because kids want to talk to their biological parents and biological parents want to respond.

● **Kids in stepfamilies feel very different from kids in first-time families** and often feel very different from adults. There are always loyalty binds in that children equate love for a stepparent with betrayal of biological parents. Children experience overwhelming change and loss—previous parent, childhood home, the very center of the thing that holds them together, their family. Even if their home and furniture is the same, the family isn't—one of their biological parents is missing at the dinner table.

When a new partner enters the family, kids are often suddenly more excluded. In our culture, this change often registers largely with girls; whereas boys may get a buddy in the stepdad, girls may be more threatened. Typically the mother turns her attention to her new partner and spends less one-to-one time with her daughter. Highly emotional conflict between mother and daughter often emerges when a stepfather enters the picture.

● **One thing that works for stepfamilies is compartmentalization:** spending one-to-one time in all stepfamily pairs (stepparent and biological parent, biological parent and child, stepparent and step-child).

6. Distribute **Stepfamily Perspectives** worksheets to all participants (including children) and introduce the concept of perspective in families.

● Now that we've heard a bit about typical stepfamily dynamics, it's time to look more closely at your family, explore your own experiences and feelings, and listen to the perspectives of family members in different roles from yours.

● **A stepfamily is a family structure in which members have very different experiences from each other.** It's like the metaphor of three blind people feeling an elephant's body. Depending on their position, they will experience the elephant differently. The one by the trunk might describe it as long and skinny and movable. The one by the back leg will experience something thick and sturdy like a tree trunk. The one near the tusk will describe something smooth and hard and sharp. Stepfamily members have very different experiences in the family because each family position creates a very different perspective and set of feelings.

➤ Use your worksheet to help you begin describing your perspective of your stepfamily elephant.

➢ You will have 6 minutes to fill this sheet out as fully as you can. Be as honest as possible without criticizing yourself. Nobody will see this but you.

➢ For people who don't like to write, use these questions to think about your experiences in your stepfamily. Feel free to draw pictures or cartoons that express what you feel.

7. When 6 minutes have passed, invite participants to share experiences and feelings with others, in a sequence of three discussions.

➤ The next thing we are going to do is to talk about *what ever people feel comfortable sharing* of what they wrote down. Our goal is to learn some more about the feelings of each stepfamily role. So we are going to share in three groups: First the children will share. Then the stepparents, and then the biological parents.

☞ *In a brief educational experience, allow 5–10 minutes for each goldfish bowl and 5–10 minutes for questions from the outer circle, for a total of 15–30 minutes.*

In a longer therapeutic workshop context, allow 15–20 minutes for each goldfish bowl, and 10 (absolute minimum) to 20 minutes for questions from the outer circle, for a total of 25–40 minutes per round. All three goldfish bowls will take 75–120 minutes, or more if you are running a full day workshop.

8. For the first round, ask for four or five *children* to volunteer to be in the center. If your group is small, ask all children who are willing to come into the center of the room. Ask the adults to sit in a circle around them.

➤ Children sit in a circle in the center of the room.

➢ Take turns talking about your answers to the questions on the worksheet, telling whatever you feel comfortable sharing.

➢ Listen to each other carefully. Do not interrupt or criticize.

➤ Adults sit in a circle around the children.

➢ Folks on the outside, your job is to listen carefully to the discussion and see what you can learn.

➢ Do not interrupt, even if you have a different point of view. Be careful not to send critical or disapproving nonverbal messages.

☞ *If you have a shorter amount of time, you can ask each goldfish bowl member to share just one thing that stands out for them* *about what they wrote. Or you can ask participants to talk about **whatever they feel comfortable sharing** of their answers to either Questions 1 and 2, Questions 3 and 4, or Questions 5 and 6 on the **Stepfamily Perspectives** worksheet. If you have more time, you could ask each goldfish bowl member to take 3 or 4 minutes to share three or four things from their worksheet.*

9. When children have had the chance to share experiences and feelings call time. Thank the children for being so generous and brave. Invite stepparents and biological parents to respond to two things:

    ✓ What would you say was one thing you have learned listening to the children?

    ✓ Are there any questions stepparents or biological parents would like to ask of the children?

10. Thank all for being so respectful. Then invite stepparents into the center and repeat *Steps 8* and *9,* with biological parents and children sitting on the outside, listening carefully to the stepparents without interrupting or sending nonverbal messages.

11. Finally, invite biological parents into the center and repeat *Steps 8* and *9,* with stepparents and children sitting on the outside, listening carefully to the biological parents without interrupting or sending nonverbal messages.

12. After children, stepparents, and biological parents have had a turn in the goldfish bowl, ask everyone to return to their seats. Invite questions, observations, insights, resolutions. Use these as opportunities to reinforce key points.

13. End the workshop with an affirmation of learning, inviting participants in pairs, family groups, or the large group to share responses to the sentence, "I learned that . . . "

VARIATION

▒ Instead of using goldfish bowls, ask family members to interview each other about responses to the last two items on the worksheet. Or have workshop members interview each other for 15 minutes in pairs, mixing people from different families. Reconvene the group and ask members to spend 15 minutes to share what they have learned.

Submitted by Patricia L. Papernow, EdD, and adapted from exercises in her invaluable book about stepfamily development, Becoming a Stepfamily: Patterns of Development in Remarried Families *(San Francisco, CA: Jossey-Bass Publisher, 1993).*

STEPFAMILY PERSPECTIVES

1. One of my early fantasies was . . .

2. What turned out to be the reality was . .

3. The wish or fantasy I can let go of more easily is . . .

4. The ones harder for me to relinquish are . . .

5. The feelings that have been the most painful or confusing to me in my stepfamily are . . .

6. What has been nicest or most pleasing for me is . . .

(800) 247-6789

12 SINGLE PARENT HIERARCHY OF NEEDS

This quick and easy needs assessment will help single parents identify current needs, see where these needs fall on Maslow's classic hierarchy of needs scale, and explore strategies for meeting these needs.

GOALS

To assess current needs as a single parent and discover how these compare to Maslow's hierarchy of needs.

To identify possibilities for meeting personal and family needs.

GROUP SIZE

Unlimited.

TIME FRAME

40–50 minutes.

MATERIALS NEEDED

Single Parent Hierarchy of Needs worksheet; newsprint; markers; list of resources for single parents.

PROCESS

Prepare and duplicate a list of local, state, and national resources that may be useful to single parents (social services, counseling agencies, child support services, legal aid, parenting classes, support groups, mentoring programs, Parents Anonymous, community health clinics, transitional housing, women's coalition, food shelf, etc.).

1. Start with a short get-acquainted exercise focused on the positives and negatives of single parenting. (2–4 minutes)

    ➤ Pair up with someone you do not know well and share your responses to these two statements:

      ➤ The best thing about single parenting is . . .
      ➤ The worst thing about single parenting is . . .

2. Solicit examples of the best and worst aspects of single parenting and list them in *best* and *worst* columns on newsprint or a blackboard.

3. Incorporate participants' comments into a chalktalk summarizing the benefits and risks of single parenting.

● **Single parenting can be an incredibly gratifying experience**, giving children and adults surprising gifts and deeply satisfying experiences. Single parenting definitely has benefits:

○ **Flexible role models for kids.** Because single parents manage responsibilities traditionally assigned to both parents, children are less constrained by traditional definitions of male and female roles. When they see the versatile and flexible roles assumed by their parent, they are more likely to grow up trusting that many choices are open to them, independent of gender.

○ **Single parents can focus without distraction on the needs of their kids.** If you are not torn between paying attention to children or to your partner, you can relate to your kids in less conflicted ways. This gives children the clarity they need. It's easier to make decisions because you don't have to consult with someone—and kids don't get mixed messages.

○ **Single parenting can bring out positive qualities you never knew you had.** Single parents are surprised and delighted by the depth of feeling they have for their children, biological and adopted. Single parents often comment that their kids challenged and stretched them to become more than they ever thought they could be.

○ **Parenting can provide a sense of direction during tumultuous times** and provide a balance to a life too centered on career. Mothering or fathering can nurture your soul, give you purpose and meaning.

○ **Raising kids alone can be the solution, not the problem.** Ongoing family conflict and turmoil is unhealthy for children. If adult relationship problems cannot be resolved, single parenting can be a means of restoring peace and stability in the home, creating an atmosphere conducive to healthy child development.

○ **Single-parenting can save you and your children from a path of destruction.** You may not have been able to leave an abusive relationship to save yourself, but when it became clear that your children were in danger, you found the courage to leave. This decision may have saved each person's life or health.

● **Single-parenting is also probably the toughest job you've ever had.** Consider some of the stresses unique to single parenting.

○ **Relentless demands.** All parents are subject to constant interruptions and requests for attention. Children need you *now*.

The relentlessness of these demands is even more acute for single parents. There is never enough time to take care of all the responsibilities you must handle.

No time for me. Many single parents are chronically exhausted from juggling multiple responsibilities. It's tough to find time (or money) to take a vacation, go to a movie, read a good book, or just relax.

Demands of work and needs of children may conflict. How can you maintain your credibility at work when you can't be as flexible and available as your colleagues or coworkers? It's especially tough if your employer makes impossible scheduling demands such as breakfast meetings or weekend retreats. When you're at work, you think of your kids at home; when at home, you think of unfinished work. It's a constant struggle for single parents to balance the two.

The main challenge is often money. Child support payments— if you ever got them—are going down every year. It's a struggle to keep your family supplied with groceries, rent, utilities, clothes, school supplies—let alone have enough for those special treats you'd love to give your children—movies, toys, etc.

You don't have a partner to share your burdens. It would be great to have another adult in the house to rely on when your kids are sick or when you're overwhelmed. And there's no one to share the joy with or the pleasure of watching your kids grow.

It's hard to have a social life. Most of the time you're too tired to go out, even if you do have the money to hire a baby-sitter. Or you may want to go out, but cannot afford child care. You need friends and a social life to stay mentally healthy, so child care is a very important issue needing your attention.

4. Acknowledge that not every single parent has the same issues or needs; each person has unique circumstances and family dynamics. Give a short explanation about Maslow's hierarchy.

   Draw as you describe. Personalize the presentation with lots of examples highlighting special needs of single parents.

   Psychologist Abraham Maslow observed that **our behavior is always geared toward meeting needs.** His pyramid model reflects his theory that human beings must satisfy primary needs such as survival and safety before they are free to pursue less essential directions such as personal fulfillment.

- Single parents are often suddenly thrown back into the **survival mode,** struggling to meet needs at the base of Maslow's pyramid after years of functioning at other levels. This shift can be very disconcerting.

- **Physical needs** (food, water, air, heat, sex) form the base of Maslow's pyramid because they are essential to sustain life. Once these necessities are assured, you are free to explore the next level of needs.

- **Safety and security** represent concrete *physical* things you need to keep yourself and your children from harm: shelter, clothes, a safe environment, protection from an abusive ex-partner, and perhaps money to pay for these things. If you can meet these needs adequately, there may be time and energy to move to the next level.

- **Social needs** represent your need to belong to a group or social system like a family where you can interact with others and give and receive support and stimulation. Connections with people are very important for well-being. From the context of this social network of adult conversation and companionship, you are free to seek to satisfy more personal needs.

- **Self-esteem** refers to our need to feel worthwhile, competent, lovable, respected, recognized, understood, and accepted. All people—adults and children—have this need, but your daily physical, safety, security, and social needs must be met before you can afford the luxury of worrying about self-esteem.

- **Self-actualization** is at the tip of the pyramid. It refers to your need to grow and develop, to find meaning in your life, to fulfill your dreams, to reach your potential, to be the best person you can be. It's hard to do this when you're hungry or worrying about how to pay the rent—so basic needs take priority. Unfortunately, self-actualization is more of a dream than a reality for most single parents.

5. Distribute the **Single Parent Hierarchy of Needs** worksheets and invite everyone to explore their current needs on the hierarchy. (2–3 minutes)

   - Read through the needs listed in each of the five levels of Maslow's hierarchy and consider how the pyramid applies to your life as a single parent.

   - Start with the bottom level of the pyramid and move upward.

> *Cross out* any need that is met to your satisfaction right now.
> *Circle* unfulfilled needs or those you have difficulty satisfying.
> Add relevant personal needs you are aware of in any section.

6. When most people have identified their needs, invite them to reflect on the *potency* or *importance* of their needs according to Maslow's hierarchy.

   > Look over your worksheet. Do your unmet needs fall into the basic categories (physical, safety/security, social) or in the higher order needs for esteem and personal growth?

      > Do not judge yourself. Accept and respect yourself and your needs, whatever they are, no matter where they fall on the hierarchy, no matter how many you have.

   > When most people have identified their needs, invite participants to pair up with a neighbor and talk about their pattern of unmet needs. (3–5 minutes)

7. Solicit examples of needs participants identified and comment briefly on the group themes and individual similarities and dissimilarities.

8. Invite the group to consider possible strategies single parents could use to meet their needs. Acknowledge that there are not many alternatives in meeting physical needs. Brainstorm two or three general approaches or specific strategies in meeting needs in each of the other four levels.

9. Divide participants into four small groups to brainstorm additional ideas and strategies for meeting their needs in the different levels of the hierarchy.

   > *Have people number off by fours. Designate an area of the room for each group to meet and assign one of Maslow's top four need levels to each group.*

10. Give each group newsprint and a marker and provide guidelines for brainstorming. (4–6 minutes)

    > Appoint a group recorder to keep track of ideas generated and to report for your group.

    > Take 4 minutes to brainstorm ideas for how a single parent could meet some of the needs in your assigned section of the pyramid.

       > Be creative, include ideas which may seem outrageous or wild.
       > Do not judge, criticize, or censor anyone's ideas. Include all suggestions, regardless of whether you agree with them or not.

> ☞ *Eavesdrop on the brainstorming. If any group seems to get stuck or off track, offer some concrete examples from the lists on page 82.*

11. When group energy seems to be winding down, interrupt the discussions and invite group reporters to take turns sharing their idea lists.

> ☞ *Ask reporters to come to the front of the room to give their reports. Hang the lists so they are visible to all participants.*

12. Summarize ideas presented by each group, hand out resource lists, and conclude with a short chalktalk affirming the individual and collective strengths of single parents in the room.

● **Celebrate your accomplishments** in meeting some of your family's critical needs. Identify one or two ideas you'd like to act on in the weeks ahead to meet additional needs.

● **Remember to affirm yourself as a single parent.** Focus on the positives which you identified as the best parts of being a single parent. Notice your successes in meeting your own needs as well as the needs of your children. You can take pride in what you are doing, in the efforts you are making, and in the role-model you are giving your children.

SINGLE PARENT HIERARCHY OF NEEDS List

Self-actualization needs

Develop a career; take risks; go back to school; create something (write a poem or story, paint a picture, write a book, invent a new product, sing, dance, or act); attend creative arts; develop a talent; learn a new skill; start a business; become physically fit; gain understanding and wisdom; advance in my job; travel to a new place; go on a wonderful adventure; follow up on a personal goal; clarify my values.

Self-esteem needs

Develop pride; affirm myself; accept myself; learn to be comfortable alone; enjoy my own company; stop judging and criticizing myself; forgive myself; let go of shame about past mistakes or hurts; celebrate my uniqueness; laugh and play more often; accept my body as it is; celebrate my gifts as a parent; accept compliments; feel worthwhile; accept and assert my personal rights; receive recognition; gain prestige.

Social needs

See my friends more often; have contact with grandparents or foster grandparents; develop new friendships; find a mentor; explore big brother/big sister programs for my children; renew or develop connections with my family of origin; have lunch with someone I like; join a support group; belong to an organization; do volunteer work; get involved at my children's school; go to church; vote; work on a community development project; practice teamwork on my job; plan more social activities; invite friends to my home; get to know my neighbors; practice inclusiveness in all my relationships; join a hobby club or an interest group; have a job; develop a passion about something outside myself; take political or social action; attend a parenting class; get to know my children's friends or their friend's parents; move into town or a new neighborhood; find other people like me (adoptive single parents, gays and lesbians, blacks, American Indians, etc.); seek companionship; make connections in a neighborhood; pursue friendships with my colleagues at work.

Physical security and safety needs

Safe and affordable housing; housing with enough space for my family; locks for my doors and windows; a good porch light; a safe home and neighborhood; an order for protection to keep my husband or boyfriend away; a working telephone; clothing (adult, child, baby); diapers; enough income to pay my bills and live securely; health insurance; movement or exercise; working smoke alarms; fire exits from my home; a plan for emergency fire escape; a fire extinguisher; a door peephole; safe appliances, including a working furnace; curtains, doors, windowshades, fences, or other physical boundaries to give me privacy; gentle, nonviolent touch; furniture, including beds and blankets; transportation; insurance for my vehicle; information about emergency first aid; preventive medicine (vitamins, immunizations); self-defense skills; a child-proof home; stair gates; a safety leash for my toddler; strollers; parenting skills; anger management skills; a friend or relative who can provide relief when I am stressed and at risk for abusing my kids; Parents' Anonymous support group; tools and other resources for maintaining and repairing my home or apartment; predictability in my day-to-day life.

SINGLE PARENT HIERARCHY OF NEEDS

SELF-ACTUALIZATION NEEDS

• personal growth •
• optimizing potential •
• finding meaning • achieving
dreams • continuing education•

SELF-ESTEEM NEEDS

• competence • acceptance •
• understanding • respect • recognition/affirmation •
• confidence • sense of worth • accomplishment •

SOCIAL NEEDS

• belonging • connection • affection •
• support • stimulation • conversation • companionship •

PHYSICAL SECURITY AND SAFETY NEEDS

• shelter • clothing • safe environment • health care •

PHYSICAL NEEDS

• food • water • warmth • breathable air • sex •

13 GAY AND LESBIAN ISSUES

This facilitated group discussion provides an opportunity for participants to gain information and explore feelings about gay and lesbian issues.

GOALS

To become familiar with some of the issues that affect the lives of gay, lesbian, and bisexual individuals and families.

To explore the personal attitudes and beliefs about different sexual orientations.

GROUP SIZE

5–25 participants.

TIME FRAME

60–90 minutes.

MATERIALS NEEDED

Chalkboard or newsprint; marker; a set of 3" x 5" **Issue Cards** (prepared ahead of time); list of local resources and reading list (compiled by trainer) for each participant.

PROCESS

This exercise assumes that you have worked through your own homophobia, are familiar with gay and lesbian issues, and are aware of your personal attitudes and values on these issues.

*Use the **Gay and Lesbian Issues** list on pages 88 and 89 and 3"x 5" notecards to create **Issue Cards** for Step 5. Write a different **Question/ Statement** on each card (the **Answers** are to assist you in facilitating discussion). Mark the back of one of the cards with a star for Step 6. Add one or two blank cards to the deck to serve as "wild cards."*

Compile a list of local or state and national resources on gay and lesbian concerns, including gay hotlines, bookstores, and religious, social, and political organizations. Include some references for further reading.

1. Start by asking everyone to sit in a circle so they can see and hear each other. Then introduce yourself and invite others to do the same.

2. Create a safe environment for discussion and learning by establishing

a few ground rules for the session. Write each ground rule on the board as you explain it to the group.

- **Respect**. Everyone deserves to be treated with respect, regardless of whether or not you agree with their beliefs.
- **Nonjudgmental acceptance.** Individuals may be at different places in examining their views about homosexuality. We need a place where folks can acknowledge their own biases without fear of judgment from others.
- **Confidentiality**. The information learned in the session may certainly be discussed outside it, but personal information regarding the participants should be treated as confidential.

3. Invite folks to participate in a short icebreaker.

   ➤ Pair up with someone you do not know and spend 3 or 4 minutes discussing what you hope to learn from this workshop.

4. Reconvene the group and ask for volunteers to share what they want to get out of the workshop experience. List questions, expectations, and hopes of participants on the board or newsprint as they are shared. Indicate which of these will be part of the workshop and which are beyond the scope of the session's discussion.

5. Distribute the **Issue Cards** around the circle, one per person. Then provide guidelines for group discussion and ask for a volunteer to go first.

   It's okay if some people don't have a card; everyone will have a chance to participate in the discussion. Depending on the size of the group and the time available, you may need to limit the amount of time spent on any one card.

   ➤ Read the statement or question on the card aloud so that everyone can hear.

   ➤ Start the discussion by responding to what is on your card; either by answering the question, presenting another viewpoint, refuting the statement, or supporting the information given.

   ➤ Other participants, join in the discussion with additional perspectives, information, etc.

   ➤ If you receive a blank card, you may ask any question you wish.

   At relevant points in the discussion, expand on key topics (coming out, the costs of staying in the closet, homophobia, and heterosexism). Use the information listed after each issue statement to supplement participant-generated discussion. Try to relate all comments to participants' expectations as recorded earlier.

6. Use the starred card to provoke a group simulation about exclusion. At some point in the discussion (if conversation lulls or folks seem to want a change of pace), draw attention to the card with a star by asking if anyone noticed anything different about any of the cards.

   When someone points out the card with the star, ask the person holding that card if she was aware that her card was different. If so, at what point did she become aware of the difference? How did she feel about the difference? Ask others in the group what they thought of the card with the star. Then talk about differences.

   - **Being gay or lesbian means being different from most people.** Sometimes others may notice the difference before the person understands that difference or is ready to acknowledge it.

   - **Differences are often not valued.** Children and adolescents often feel tremendous pressure to *fit in*, to conform. Adults may be wary or suspicious of people who are different.

   - **People who are different tend to be marginalized.** Growing up feeling different from everyone else can lead to feelings of isolation and loneliness. People who feel different often seek out others who share their difference and avoid the majority, who may not value or accept them.

7. Return to the general discussion of issues by asking another participant to read an **Issue Card.** Continue the discussion until there are 10–15 minutes left in the session. Then draw the current discussion to a close and ask if people have any questions that have not yet been answered. If possible, respond to these questions directly.

   - *Tell the group that the workshop has been a start to answering some of the questions they may have had. It may have raised some more questions in their minds. Hopefully, in the course of the discussion, they have developed some comfort in talking about gay and lesbian issues. Encourage them to continue these discussions in the future with others (friends and family members, gay and lesbian individuals, helping professionals).*

8. Remind the group of the number of people affected by gay and lesbian issues and the importance of supporting gay and lesbian people.

   - **One in ten people in the United States are gay or lesbian.**

Millions of families are touched by these issues. Today, many or most people know someone gay or have a relative or close friend who is gay. It is often easier to never mention these relatives, or to brush over gay persons. We live in a *don't ask, don't tell* culture —and many gay and lesbian people never come out to their family or friends because of the great fear of losing the support they need.

● **Support of family and friends is very important.** Experts estimate that one-third of all victims of youth suicide are gay. Not having the support of your family at a time when you are most vulnerable can affect you the rest of your life.

9. Talk about the ways nongay people can become supportive allies in gay and lesbian people's struggle for acceptance. Ask participants for ideas about things they could do to become gay allies and chart the answers on the board.

The list might include activities such as:
Joining organizations like P-FLAG (Parents, Families, and Friends of Lesbians and Gays)
Attending a gay pride parade or festival
Writing to elected officials about relevant legislation
Expressing disapproval of antigay jokes
Teaching children that it's not okay to attack people who are different
Using inclusive language
Supporting gay-owned businesses
Supporting tolerance-based education programs in schools
Asking congregations to become welcoming or affirming of gays

10. Hand out the prepared reading list and resource list and point out where materials are available in your area (library, gay center, alternative bookstore, mail order, gay and lesbian bookstores).

Two excellent books you can recommend are Don Clark's Loving Someone Gay *(Celestial Arts: Berkeley, California, 1987) and Brian McNaught's* On Being Gay *(St. Martin's Press: New York, 1988). For parents of gays and lesbians, we recommend Betty Fairchild and Nancy Hayward's* Now That You Know: What Every Parent Should Know About Homosexuality *(New York: Harcourt Brace Jovanovich, 1989).*

Contributed by Andy King.

© 1997 Whole Person Associates 210 W Michigan Duluth, MN 55802   (800) 247-6789

GAY AND LESBIAN ISSUES

Q: Do gay people really have some kind of sixth sense that allows them to identify other gay people?
A: Gay, lesbian, and bisexual people may look for subtle clues about the sexual orientation of others that nongay people often overlook.

Q: My daughter told me she was a lesbian. Where did I go wrong?
A: Once could also ask, "How do people become heterosexual?" There is still much to be learned about the development of sexual orientation, but current research indicates at least some genetic basis for homosexuality.

Q: There is no such thing as a bisexual, only people who are afraid to admit that they are really gay.
A: For decades, research has shown that people self-identify along a continuum of sexual orientations, from exclusively heterosexual to exclusively homosexual, with many people somewhere in between.

Some people who are bisexual are attracted to members of both sexes at the same point in their lives; others may experience a stronger attraction to one sex during one period of time and then to the other sex at another period of their lives.

Q: Gays are alienating straight people by demanding all these "special rights."
A: Most of the legislation proposed by gay and lesbian advocacy groups is designed to protect gays and lesbians from discrimination or to provide the same benefits or rights that heterosexuals enjoy.

Q: Why does my gay son feel the need to "come out" to people? Can't he just go about his private life without having to tell everyone what he does?
A: Coming out is a crucial event in the lives of gay, lesbian, and bisexual people. It is a point at which they define who they are to themselves and others.

Coming out to others is about letting people know who you are as a person. It takes tremendous energy to pretend to be someone you're not. Even simple questions such as, "What did you do last weekend?" could be threatening if you don't know how the person asking would react to knowing that you're gay.

Q: If I "come out" at work, I could lose my job.
A: In most states, it is legal to fire someone simply because he or she is gay or lesbian. Very few states have legislation that prevents gay people from being fired unfairly.

Employees should be able to focus on their work and shouldn't have to spend time and energy constantly worrying about getting fired for who they are.

Q: People who plan to come out should think of the embarrassment they will cause their family.
A: Many people have a friend or family member who is gay or lesbian, but because it's not something that can be seen, they may never know it. Often, learning that a family member is gay or lesbian can be a challenge. But, with some information, support, and a little time, families can become tremendously supportive and find no reason to be embarrassed.

Q: Most gay-bashing would not have occurred if the person would have acted straight.
A: Blaming the victim is a common way of sidestepping the issue of bigotry and hatred and avoiding responsibility for perpetrating violence against others.

Q: Two people living together is okay, but asking the state to legalize same sex marriage is taking things too far.
A: Married people enjoy benefits that others don't (for example, inclusion in family health insurance plans), and these benefits are not available to same-sex couples.

Q: Gay parents should not tell their children they are gay until the kids are at least eighteen.

A: Children are much more perceptive than adults often realize. Treating sexual orientation as a secret communicates to children that there must be something wrong with it. Age-appropriate discussions will help children to understand who their parents are.

Q: Same-sex couples should not be allowed to adopt because the child would suffer the stigma of having gays for parents.

A: If we buy into this type of thinking, then it would follow that black couples should not have children because they would suffer the effects of racism. The problem is not having two parents of the same sex, but society's prejudice.

Q: Allowing gays in the military would undermine morale and put our national security at risk.

A: Despite the tremendous efforts and expense invested by the military to remove them, gays and lesbians have served in the military throughout history, often achieving high rank and commendation. Discharging people because of who they are is more likely to undermine morale and perpetuate bigotry.

Q: Gays should not be allowed to teach in our schools; children are so impressionable.

A: Children are impressionable and learn that antigay bigotry is okay when they see their school fire qualified teachers because of their sexual orientation.

Q: The schools have no business promoting homosexuality.

A: Adolescents who committed violence against gays said they thought it was okay because no one (not their parents, their school, nor the church) ever told them it was wrong to do so. They learned that homosexuality was "bad" and so thought nothing was wrong with attacking a person they perceived as gay.

Most gays and lesbians first become aware of their sexual orientations as teenagers, and most gay and lesbian teens do not receive support at this time when they most need it.

Q: What is homophobia?

A: Homophobia is an irrational fear or hatred of homosexuals or homosexuality. (This doesn't refer to being uncomfortable with something that you're unfamiliar with.)

Like all prejudice, homophobia is learned.

Homophobia is based in sexism and misogyny. A society that does not value women and traits associated with them will also not value men who exhibit "feminine" traits. Similarly, women who are sexually unavailable to men are seen as a threat to male dominance.

Homophobia is manifested in many ways: personal beliefs and actions (gay-bashing), institutional policies (ban against gays in the military), and societal rules and laws (prohibition against same-sex marriage).

Heterosexism is the assumption that everyone is heterosexual or that everyone should be. Heterosexual privilege consists of the rights and benefits available to heterosexuals that are denied gays and lesbians (right to marry, right to spousal insurance benefits, right to inherit property, right to make medical decisions, etc.).

Q: Homosexuality must be some sort of psychological disorder. Look at how prevalent alcoholism, depression, and suicide are among gay people.

A: The high rates of chemical dependency, depression, and suicide in the gay community are related to society's lack of acceptance of gay people.

14 PLAYING FOR INTIMACY

Couples will love this lighthearted exploration of the connection between play and intimacy, which helps them realize that there are many roads to intimacy and one of the most joyful ones is play.

GOALS

To understand the relationship between play and intimacy.

To learn new facets of intimacy and explore ways to develop these in relationship with a partner.

To identify barriers to play and create strategies for overcoming them.

GROUP SIZE

Unlimited.

TIME FRAME

60–90 minutes.

MATERIALS NEEDED

Relationship Intimacy worksheet; blank paper; newsprint; marker.

PROCESS

> *This exercise was written for intimate adult partners, but could be easily adapted for families by eliminating sexual intimacy from the process.*

1. Start with an icebreaker to help people get acquainted. (5–8 minutes)
   > Pair up with another couple to form a group of four and find a place to sit down together.

   > Take turns talking about how you learned to play. You each have 2 minutes to share.

2. Invite folks to share reasons for coming to a play workshop; weave participant interests into a group agenda; and establish ground rules for safety (confidentiality, acceptance, respect, etc.).
   - **It is important that you feel safe when you play.** You need to know that you will not be hurt, belittled, put down, judged, or rejected. Trust is essential: trust in yourself, your partner, and other people. When you feel trusting, you are more able to play freely and spontaneously, without holding back or worrying about consequences.

3. Invite couples to revisit some of their early play experiences and recall what was special about them. Distribute blank paper and guide couples in a reflection on playfulness in their relationship. (6–8 minutes)

> Find a place in the room where you can sit together privately.

> Make a list of special, playful times that you shared when your relationship was younger.

~ Recall specific times or events when you really enjoyed being together. Try to think of at least four or five different events or play experiences.

~ Write a short description of each event.

> For each event, write a statement about what made it so good or special.

  Solicit examples.

4. Ask couples to share facets of their play experiences that made them special or memorable, noting the rebellious element in play.

● **Play often involves some form of rebellion** or breaking the rules. When you play, you break out of standard, socially acceptable forms of behavior and do something spontaneous: throw food across the table at your spouse, stick your tongue out at a pompous salesman when he turns his back, giggle in church, etc.

5. Present the Metz model for the developmental relationship between play and intimacy. Explain the meaning of each type of play and intimacy as you go.

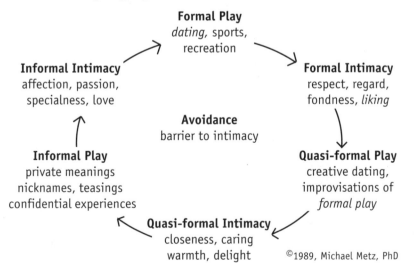

Formal Play
dating, sports,
recreation

Informal Intimacy
affection, passion,
specialness, love

Formal Intimacy
respect, regard,
fondness, *liking*

Avoidance
barrier to intimacy

Informal Play
private meanings
nicknames, teasings
confidential experiences

Quasi-formal Play
creative dating,
improvisations of
formal play

Quasi-formal Intimacy
closeness, caring
warmth, delight

©1989, Michael Metz, PhD

☞ *Copy this model on newsprint or a blackboard and use it for illustration during your chalktalk, making sure to inform participants that it was developed and copyrighted by Dr. Michael Metz.*

Start with a definition of formal play and work clockwise around the diagram, ending with informal intimacy. Elaborate on how play leads to intimacy, which leads to more play and more intimacy.

● **Formal play** is usually some form of dating, sports, or recreation, like going out to dinner or playing a game of tennis. This type of play is fairly standard and predictable and conforms to social norms.

● **Formal intimacy** often results from formal play: feelings of respect, regard, fondness, and liking for your partner, which are a result of your having spent structured time together.

● **Quasi-formal play** is a natural result of establishing formal intimacy. Once you like and respect your partner, you are more likely to get creative when you date and to improvise on the formal play of your early relationship. For example, when you enjoy the formal play of skiing, you might now engage in a spontaneous snowball fight or a race to the bottom of the hill.

● **Quasi-formal intimacy.** Quasi-formal play leads to quasi-formal intimacy. This refers to feelings of closeness, caring, warmth, and delight created by your quasi-formal play together.

● **Informal play.** Informal play grows out of quasi-formal intimacy. You are now familiar with each other and have a history of special, confidential experiences which have private meanings for you and your partner. You might have affectionate nicknames for each other and engage in teasings that are personal to you as a couple.

● **Informal Intimacy.** Informal play leads to informal intimacy or expressions of affection, passion, specialness, and love based on previous play experiences, shared history, and trust.

6. Invite people to ask questions about the model, then ask participants to guess how many types of intimacy there are. Announce that there are twelve facets of intimacy which you will briefly describe.

    ☞ *Elaborate on each point, sprinkle colorful examples throughout, or ask participants to share their own examples of each.*

● **Recreation:** Sharing experiences of fun, sports, hobbies, recreation; sharing ways of refilling the wells of energy, leisure.

● **Aesthetic:** Sharing experiences of beauty—music, nature, art, theater, dance, movies; drinking from the common cup of beauty.

Intellectual: Sharing the world of ideas, a genuine touching of persons based on mutual respect for each other's intellectual capacities (reading, discussing, respectful debating, etc.).

Commitment: Togetherness derived from dedication to a common cause, value, or effort (working for a political cause).

Work: Sharing common tasks or projects, supporting each other in bearing responsibilities (raising a family, house/yard chores, etc.).

Communication: Being open, honest, trusting, truthful, loving; giving constructive feedback; positive confrontation.

Crisis: Standing together in the major and minor tragedies which persist in life; closeness in coping with problems and pain.

Sexual: Sensual-emotional satisfaction, the experience of sharing and self-abandon in the physical merging of two persons; sensual-sexual fantasies and desires.

Emotional: Depth awareness and sharing of significant meanings and feelings; the touching of your innermost selves.

Creative: Helping each other to grow, to be cocreators (not reformers) of each other.

Conflict: Standing-up with and to each other, fighting in nondestructive ways, facing and struggling with differences.

Spiritual: The *we-ness* of sharing ultimate concerns, meanings of life, philosophies, and religious experience.

7. Invite people to share surprise discoveries and insights or to raise questions and issues related to concepts of intimacy.

   ✔ Were you surprised by any of the twelve facets of intimacy?

   ✔ Did one or two avenues of intimacy stand out as your favorites and others as your least favorite?

   > *Use this time to emphasize the point that individuals have different desires for avenues of closeness, that one is not inherently better than another, that deficits in one area can be balanced with strengths in another.*

8. Distribute the **Relationship Intimacy** worksheets to participants and invite people to explore preferred avenues for closeness and their satisfaction with relationship intimacy on each of these twelve aspects. (5–6 minutes)

   ➤ First, rank each of the twelve facets of intimacy according to its *importance to you.*

~ Use the number 1 for the most important facet for you, a 2 for the next most important, and so on with 12 being least important.

~ Write your **Importance Ranking** in the space provided at the left.

~ Remember, everyone's rankings will be different!

☞ *Make sure rankings are done by all before moving on.*

➤ Now describe your current degree of satisfaction with each facet of intimacy in your relationship.

~ Use a scale of 0–10, with 0 = very low satisfaction and 10 = very high satisfaction.

~ Write your **Satisfaction Level** with each facet in the space provided at the right.

9. Invite participants to share intimacy priorities and satisfaction levels with their partners. (4–5 minutes)

➤ Take turns with your partner. Share your discoveries about desire for and satisfaction with aspects of intimacy in your current relationship.

~ Maintain a respectful, nonjudgmental attitude. This is an opportunity to increase intimacy by learning more about your partner. Avoid personal attack, criticism, or blaming of your partner for any disappointments or frustrations you may be feeling in your relationship.

~ Partners listen carefully, without interrupting, seeking to hear and understand your partner's perceptions and feelings.

~ You each have 2 minutes to share your discoveries and insights.

10. Reconvene the group and ask for examples of facets of intimacy couples are interested in developing. As areas are named, invite everyone to brainstorm ideas for enhancing that area of intimacy through play. Write all ideas on newsprint or on the blackboard.

11. Ask participants to reflect on what might interfere with the ability to act on these playful ideas or fully enjoy playful experiences with partners. Record barriers on another newsprint and hang it beside the list of playful ideas.

☞ *If necessary, prime the pump (embarrassment, fear of rejection or ridicule, belief that play is immature or irresponsible, lack of trust, restrictive early learnings, lack of leisure/free time, fatigue, fear of intimacy, power/control issues, trauma, insufficient leadership, etc.).*

12. Acknowledge the validity of these barriers and address them in a chalktalk on how to enhance playfulness and develop intimacy.

- **Be convinced of the absolute value of play.** Acknowledge how past play experiences have become a special part of your relationship history and created desired closeness with your partner. Look for these positive benefits when you play with your partner.

- **Carefully work through your own inhibitions about play.** Develop your skills at:

  - **Laughter/humor.** Find your funny bone—and your partner's—and tickle it often.

  - **Fantasy.** Develop your ability to imagine joyful, funny, intimate events with your partner. Take risks to share fantasies and act on positive ones.

  - **Spontaneity.** Give yourself permission to be spontaneous, to act on impulse, to take lighthearted chances with play.

  - **Trust/risk.** If trust is an issue and it's hard for you to take risks with your partner, start by talking this over, seeking the reassurance and support you may need. Then begin slowly, starting with small, relatively safe risks—ones that you can feel fairly sure will be successful—like a phone call at work to say *Hi, I'm thinking of you*. Then, when you feel ready, move on to higher risks, like sharing feelings of love or passion.

  - **Acceptance (self/other).** Try lowering your expectations of yourself and others and focusing on your *humanity* instead. Accept yourself and your imperfections as well as your strengths and lovable qualities.

  - **Think creatively**, self-assuredly, *dangerously*—stay open to possibilities for play.

  - **Keep your play efforts warm,** lighthearted, unintimidating, and cooperative. Don't take yourself or your partner too seriously. Let go of control and your investment in the outcome of your play efforts. You don't have to *do this right, be good* at it, *prove your worth, compete* with your partner, or *be successful* every time in engaging your partner in play.

  - **Be ready with a safety net** if you pick a poor time to play. Have a plan for backing off gracefully.

  - **If after three attempts to play with your partner you receive zingers, take time to talk.** Explain your efforts to your partner and try to work out some clearer signals for playtime.

13. Invite couples to target one facet of intimacy they want to enhance through play. (5–6 minutes)

   ➤ Decide together which of the twelve facets of intimacy you'd like to develop or enhance through play and circle it.

   ➤ Decide what kind of play you want to use: formal or informal.

      ☞ *Refer back to the model of the developmental relationship between play and intimacy and review the difference between formal and informal play. Give couples time to decide.*

   ➤ Turn your worksheet over and write **Playsheet** on the top of the page. In the next 4 minutes, brainstorm as many ideas as you can for ways you might play to promote your chosen facet of intimacy.

      ➤ Remember to be wild, crazy, outrageous, funny, and deviant! The purpose is to break free of old ruts and routines and to discover new joys in playing together.

14. Reconvene the group and invite couples to share some of their playful ideas or plans for building intimacy. Conclude by reinforcing the value of playing for intimacy and the importance of making play a high priority for partner relationships.

VARIATIONS

■ Expand *Step 11* by asking partners to interview each other about their personal barriers to play using facilitative sentences like:

   ➤ Describe your painful or bad experiences at play.
   ➤ Describe your personal beliefs and fear about adult play.
   ➤ Tell about some of your personal barriers to play.

■ Ask participants to pair up with a neighbor (not their spouse/partner). Pairs interview each other about their patterns for playfulness as adults and barriers to play. Use questions such as:

   ✔ What is playful about you?
   ✔ When and where are you most playful?
   ✔ What place seems to bring out your playfulness?
   ✔ With whom are you most playful?
   ✔ What is your favorite play activity? What do you like about it?
   ✔ What is your least favorite game? What don't you like about it?

Submitted by Michael E. Metz, PhD., who designed this exercise as part of the Couples Play Workshop which he created and conducts. The twelve facets of intimacy are adapted from Howard and Doris Clinebell's pioneering work, The Intimate Marriage *(New York: Harper & Row, 1970)*

RELATIONSHIP INTIMACY

Importance   **Satisfaction**
Ranking   **Level**

Recreational Intimacy
sharing experiences of fun, sports, hobbies, recreation; sharing ways of refilling the wells of energy; leisure

Intellectual Intimacy
sharing the world of ideas; a genuine touching of persons based on mutual respect for each other's intellectual capacities (discussing, studying, etc.)

Work Intimacy
sharing common tasks, supporting each other in bearing responsibilities (raising a family, house and yard chores, etc.)

Commitment Intimacy
togetherness derived from dedication to a common cause or value (working for a political cause)

Aesthetic Intimacy
sharing experiences of beauty—music, nature, art, theater, dance, movies; drinking from the common cup of beauty

Communication Intimacy
being honest, trusting, truthful, loving; giving constructive feedback; positive confrontation

Emotional Intimacy
depth awareness and sharing of significant meanings and feelings; the touching of the innermost selves of two human beings

Creative Intimacy
helping each other to grow, to be cocreators (not reformers) of each other

Sexual Intimacy
sensual-emotional satisfaction; the experience of sharing and self-abandon in the physical merging of two persons; fantasies and desires

Crisis Intimacy
standing together in the major and minor tragedies which persist in life; closeness in coping with problems and pain

Spiritual Intimacy
the *we-ness* of sharing ultimate concerns, the meanings of life, philosophies, religious experience

Conflict Intimacy
standing-up with and to each other; facing and struggling with difference together; "fighting"

facing family problems

15 PATTERN POPPING

This thought-provoking exercise will help people realize that problematic patterns of interaction *can* be broken.

GOALS

To identify troublesome patterns of interaction in relationships with significant others.

To take steps to break those patterns and develop more constructive interactions.

GROUP SIZE

Unlimited.

TIME FRAME

60–90 minutes.

MATERIALS NEEDED

Blackboard or newsprint; blank paper; two copies of the **Pattern Popping** worksheet for each participant.

PROCESS

1. Introduce the idea of relationship patterns and distribute blank paper to everyone. Ask people to identify a common relationship pattern in their lives while giving the following directions:

    ➤ Write down an example of a common relationship pattern that you have with a family member or friend on your paper.

      — Think of a simple, everyday relationship routine that involves you and another person (you get wild and silly at parties, and your spouse tells you to quiet down; you spend too much money on fishing tackle, and your wife gets mad; your mother gets sick, and you rush in to take care of her).

2. Solicit examples of interactional patterns and how they develop and influence our mental health.

    ● **We are all creatures of habit.** Just as you gravitate toward your favorite chair in the living room, you tend to repeat roles and actions that are familiar to you (speaking up when others are quiet, cracking a joke when someone else is tense, offering care when a loved one is sick).

- **Interactional patterns are a series of mutual invitations** in which the actions of each person invites a particular response from the other. When you smile at a person, you invite that person to smile back at you. When you criticize someone, you may provoke them into pointing out *your* defects.

- **Patterns can develop a life of their own.** Patterns can be powerful enough to pull each person back into the same type of exchange over and over again, like taking the bait when your father provokes you into arguing politics. You may want to break or "pop" the pattern, but you can't seem to stop it. When this happens, *the pattern may be the problem*, not the person or the relationship.

- **Interactional patterns have a profound influence on you.** Your interactions shape your identity, self-esteem, and confidence. Did your antics on the playground win you friends at school or bring you rejection and ridicule? Your patterns, whether positive or negative, surely made a difference in how you felt about yourself then—and perhaps now.

- **There are several common interactional patterns,** including two that most people encounter in their relationships.

  - **Pursue/withdraw patterns.** Imagine a situation in which a wife feels her husband is never available to her. Perhaps he's working all the time or immersed in watching football or reading the newspaper. Her attempts to get his attention are met with increasing withdrawal. From his perspective, she continually nags him, and he feels he can never do anything right in her eyes. The more she pursues, the more he withdraws. Does this situation sound familiar?

    In this pursue/withdraw sequence the husbands withdrawing provokes his wife's pursuing and her pursuing invites his withdrawing. The pattern becomes circular and over time can take on a life of its own.

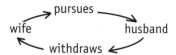

    The problem is not the husband and the problem is not the wife. The problem is the pattern. Over time, this pattern has captured them and taken a toll on their relationship.

> *Pause and raise a few reflective questions: How could this situation be described from the wife's perspective? from the husband's perspective? Ask for examples of pursuit/withdrawal patterns in other relationships.*

Overly harsh/overly soft patterns. Imagine a situation in which two parents are at odds over disciplining their son who has just taken the family car without permission and crashed it. The father wants to ground him for a month and not let him drive again for six months. The mother thinks that's too harsh and wants to ground him for a week and withhold driving privileges for a month. The father demands "What is he going to learn if we are too easy on him?" And the mother responds, "What is he going to learn if we are too hard?"

As they continue arguing, their positions become increasingly rigid. The father comes to view the mother as a cream puff and the mother comes to view the father as a drill sergeant. Can you imagine a situation like this?

This situation could be diagrammed in the following manner.

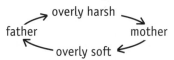

3. Engage participants in a brief discussion about this last scenario by raising several reflective questions.

   ✔ How would the mother describe this situation?
   ✔ How would the father describe this situation?
   ✔ How could you describe this situation in terms of a problematic interactional pattern?
   ✔ How do the actions of each person invite a particular response from the other?

4. Ask people what other relationship patterns they can identify. List these on newsprint, commenting on the universality of each pattern and drawing out concrete examples of the pattern in action (over-function/underfunction; minimize/maximize; criticize/defend; attack/counterattack).

5. Solicit reactions to these concepts of relationship patterns.

> *Avoid arguments about whether the real problem is in the pattern, rather than the person. Explain that this nonblaming way of looking at situations is not an attempt to describe the truth but*

simply an alternative that may be useful. Unite individuals against the pattern rather than against each other. It can be an effective first step to disrupting problematic patterns.

6. Choose a particular pattern that seems to strike a chord for participants and discuss it in more depth.

✔ What is the effect of the pattern on each person in it?

✔ What is the effect of the pattern on the relationship of the persons involved in it?

✔ What do you think the effects would be if the pattern got stronger, worse, or more frequent?

✔ What might be the effects if the pattern got weaker, better, or less frequent?

7. Distribute the **Pattern Popping** worksheets and lead people in a reflection about a particular problematic interactional pattern in their lives. Give instructions for each step of the process. (5–8 minutes)

➤ Pick a problematic interactional pattern that you're aware of in your life.

☞ *Pause after each instruction to allow time for people to record their reflections.*

– Write a brief description of the interaction from *your* perspective in the area labeled **My Perspective.**

– Write a brief description of the interaction from the *other person's* perspective in the area labeled **Other Person's Perspective.**

➤ Now focus on the pattern of interaction that occurs between you and the other person.

– Fill in the blanks of the sentence in the center of your worksheet with actions or behaviors that are a key part of your problematic relationship pattern.

☞ *Some people may have difficulty identifying their contribution to the patterns and only be able to focus on what the other person is doing. Suggest that people focus on behaviors rather than thoughts or feelings and separate the intent of a person's actions from the effect of those actions on the other person in the pattern.*

➤ What do your interactions look like?

– Use the interactional pattern diagram in the top center of your page to describe your pattern.

© 1997 Whole Person Associates 210 W Michigan Duluth, MN 55802   (800) 247-6789

> Write your own name in the circle on the left and the other person's name in the circle on the right.

> Write your action or behavior in the box on the top of the diagram. Write the action or behavior of the other person in the box at the bottom of the diagram.

> Now consider the present effects of this problematic pattern on you, the other person and your relationship, and write your responses in the **Current Effects** box.

> > What is the effect of the problematic pattern on you? What is the effect of the problematic pattern on the other person? What is the effect of the problematic pattern on your relationship?

> > What if this pattern were to continue and get worse? What would be its effects on *you?* On the *other person?* On your *relationship?*

> > Write these imagined effects if it got worse in the space for **Future Effects.**

> At the bottom of your worksheet draw another diagram of this problem pattern, showing what it would look like if it got worse.

> > *If people have trouble visualizing this, ask them to simply exaggerate their own and the other person's current behaviors and actions.*

8. Ask people to pause in their writing and reflect on their desire to change the problematic pattern.

> Would you rather that the pattern be in charge of your life or that you be in charge of the life of your pattern?

> > *While this may seem like a silly question, it is a very important one. People need to take a stand against a pattern before we support them in their efforts to stand up to it and resist its effects on them. Respect their pace.*

9. Revisit key examples of negative relationship patterns, soliciting ideas from the group on how these patterns could be interrupted and transmitted into a more positive outcome.

10. Hand out clean copies of the **Pattern Popping** worksheets and invite people to explore ways they can change their problematic interactional patterns by imagining the opposite of their *getting worse* pattern diagram. (5–8 minutes)

> Now imagine that you are going to change this problematic pattern. What would you do instead?

➤ Fill in the blanks of the sentences with new actions and behaviors for yourself and the other person.

☞ *Pause after each instruction for reflection and writing.*

➤ Describe this new pattern in the pattern diagram at the top of your worksheet.

➤ Write a brief description of the new interaction from your perspective in the box labeled **My Perspective.**

➤ Write a brief description of the new interaction from the other person's perspective in the box labeled **Their Perspective.**

➤ What would be the immediate effect of a pattern change on you? on the other person? on your relationship?

➤ Write the effects of this new interactional pattern on you, on the other person, and on the relationship in the **Current Effects** box.

➤ If this new pattern continued to strengthen, how would it affect you and your relationship?

➤ Write these imagined effects of the new pattern in the space for **Future Effects.**

➤ At the bottom or your worksheet, diagram how this new, stronger pattern might look.

11. Ask people to pair up with someone not in their family to debrief their experiences. (6–7 minutes)

➤ Take 3 minutes each to describe your insights and experience in looking at problem patterns.

☞ *To avoid having to repeat the questions, write them on a blackboard or newsprint.*

➤ Briefly describe the pattern you identified.

➤ Was it easy or hard to describe the situation as an interactional pattern? What helped you to do that?

➤ As you thought about the situation as an interactional pattern, how did it shift your sense of yourself? of the other person? of your relationship?

➤ What new thoughts did it trigger for you?

☞ *Notify people when 3 minutes are up, and it's time for the other person to share.*

12. Interrupt small group sharing and ask everyone to rejoin the large

group for a summary discussion. Invite people to give examples of patterns along with descriptions of effects of shifts in perspective. Then lead a discussion about forces working for and against changing these patterns.

✓ What things in our culture do you think support the continuation of these patterns?

✓ What suggestions would you offer others about breaking those patterns?

✓ What forces in your lives would help you in your effort to break those patterns?

13. When the discussion is winding down, summarize what has been said and weave key points into a final chalktalk, encouraging people to seek support when they are trying to pop problematic patterns.

● **Change is more likely to occur when you have support.** Changing patterns is hard work so seek needed support from your family, friends, and community network. Explore resources in your area and check support groups related to your interests and goals.

VARIATION

▨ Couples with both members present could complete worksheets separately, then pair up together for the dyad sharing as well as for working on the second exploration of possibilities for changing patterns.

This exercise was submitted by William Madsen, PhD.

© 1997 Whole Person Associates 210 W Michigan Duluth, MN 55802   (800) 247-6789

PATTERN POPPING

My
Perspective

Their
Perspective

When I do _____ it invites _____ from

the other person, and when they do _____ it invites

_____ from me.

Current Effects	**Future Effects**
	(if this pattern grew stronger)
On me . . .	On me . . .
On the other person . . .	On the other person . . .
On my relationship . . .	On my relationship . . .

16 TURN OFF THE ALARM, DEAR

This intriguing process allows couples to learn more about their partner's vulnerabilities and practice responding to their partner's emotions in a way that builds, rather than diminishes, feelings of closeness.

GOALS

To increase understanding of the personal vulnerabilities that each person brings to an intimate relationship.

To practice responding to a partner's vulnerabilities in ways that turn off personal alarm signals of distress and heighten feelings of security.

GROUP SIZE

Unlimited. Works best with at least six couples.

TIME FRAME

50–60 minutes.

MATERIALS NEEDED

Alarm Clock worksheet; newsprint; masking tape; horn or harmonica.

PROCESS

Single adults without a significant other can bring a close friend or adult family member who is committed to working on their relationship. If this is not possible, they can role-play being friends or partners with other single people in the group.

This exercise is not appropriate for couples on the verge of separating or for those experiencing physical abuse. Prescreen potential participant couples to ensure that two basic criteria for participation are met: a clear commitment to each other and to the relationship, and no history of violence in their relationship.

1. Begin by inviting people to get in touch with their feelings.

   ➤ Close your eyes and try to recall the various emotions you have felt in the last twenty-four hours.

      – Try not to judge or censor your thoughts; simply notice whatever emotions you remember: sadness, anger, fear, apprehension, joy, peacefulness, etc.

➤ When you have several feelings in mind, open your eyes.

2. Invite people to share examples of emotions they were able to get in touch with, listing these on newsprint. Then give a chalktalk defining emotions and the important role they play in relationships, especially intimate ones.

● **An emotion is a strong, complex feeling that gives you feedback** about your reactions to situations. Your emotions talk to you on several levels: in your body (*I feel butterflies in my stomach every time I have to talk in front of the group);* in your mind, where you store your rules and beliefs about emotions (*Anger is bad; I shouldn't show my feelings*); and in your emotional memory bank, where you connect emotions to your life experiences and your interpretations of these events (*Every time I try something new, I fall flat on my face and feel like a fool!*).

● **Emotions help you organize your experiences** and regulate your interactions. Your feelings signal you to behave in certain ways: to *back away* when you are afraid or in danger; *to assert yourself* when you feel put down; *to take a walk* when you're wound up and tense, *to call a friend* when you are lonely.

● **Emotions can help or hinder your relationships** depending on what you do when your emotions are aroused. If you get defensive and respond to others by *attacking/blaming* or by *withdrawing/ distancing,* this will disrupt or diminish the closeness between you. If, on the other hand, you have learned to *stay present* or *maintain emotional contact* with your partner in the face of your emotions, you are likely to heighten the intimacy and trust between you.

● **We all have internal emotional alarm clocks** that go off when past relationship wounds are activated. These alarms usually set off strong feelings like anger, fear, and sadness, and may sometimes bring out the worst in you due to the increased vulnerability you experience at these times. For example, if you often felt abandoned as a child, your internal alarm may ring every time your partner has to go out of town. Or if you have had a series of traumatic losses, your alarm might sound off every time your partner is late arriving home.

3. Invite people to reflect upon the internal *alarm buttons* that were created in their past relationship history. (3–4 minutes)

➤ Close your eyes again; take a deep breath and exhale slowly, allowing yourself to become relaxed and quiet within yourself.

> Allow yourself to travel back through time, to childhood experiences in your family home or to significant events in past relationships.

> As you sift through your life experiences, search for unfortunate or negative experiences that had a lasting impact on you, making you extra sensitive to these issues in your current relationships.

> *Offer plenty of examples:*
> *being rejected, humiliated, or put down;*
> *feeling helpless, hopeless, alone, or lonely;*
> *being smothered, controlled, or held back;*
> *being asked to do too much;*
> *being treated like you were invisible.*

> Find one or two experiences that you know have shaped your current alarm system and try to discover and name the particular danger that your alarm warns you about.

> When you have identified one or two relationship alarms, open your eyes and slowly return your attention to the room, bringing new awareness of your alarms with you into the present.

4. Give everyone an **Alarm Clock** worksheet and guide people through the process of identifying their personal alarm signals and the emotions that accompany them.

> In the space inside each of the two alarm buttons on the top of your clock, write a brief description of one or two *alarm buttons* carried from past family relationships into present intimate relationships.

> This should be a brief summary of the dangers you are trying to avoid in your present relationship (being trapped, dependent, in conflict, etc.).

> After you have identified your unique alarm signals, consider the *two primary emotions* you feel when your alarm goes off.

> Look over the various emotions appearing on the face of your alarm clock and choose the two you are most likely to feel when your alarm rings.

> Now draw in the hour and minute hands on your clock using the hour hand to point to your strongest emotion and the minute hand to point to your second most powerful feeling. This is your *emotional time*.

> Next draw in a second hand representing a third, more subtle emotion that is lurking behind the dominant, obvious emotions. This is your *second hand emotion*. It is always running around in the background when you are having an *emotional time*.

5. Invite couples to share their **Alarm Clock** responses with each other and give ground rules for the discussion.

> Take turns telling your partner what you've discovered about your *alarm buttons*, *emotional time*, and *second hand time*.

>> Tell your partner about the specific incidents or interpersonal events that shaped your alarm button.

>> Use descriptive, nonjudgmental language in telling your story, much like a reporter would report facts on the news.

>> Do not attack or blame yourself or your partner for anything that appears on your clock. It is not good or bad, it is simply your reality and should be accepted and respected.

>> The younger person of each couple should start first and spend 3 minutes interpreting their **Alarm Clock**.

> While your partner is describing their alarm buttons, listen carefully. Pay close attention to what your partner is telling you about their vulnerabilities and the emotions they feel when their alarm tells them that these sore spots are in danger of being reinjured.

>> Do not criticize, attack, or blame your partner for anything that is shared with you. Treat this as *privileged information* and try to assume an accepting and caring attitude, even if your partner's story triggers your own alarms.

> After 3–4 minutes, switch roles. The older person shares alarm buttons and the younger person listens with a caring and understanding attitude.

>> *Make sure everyone understands the ground rules. Unobtrusively monitor the conversations and intervene with gentle reminders about nonjudgmental listening, if necessary. Keep time and announce when it is time to switch roles.*

6. When couple talk seems to be winding down, interrupt the discussions and invite couples to share their discoveries with the large group, after they have asked permission from each other to do so.

> *Encourage people to check with their partner before revealing personal information about the partner to the large group so that the personal boundaries of each individual are respected.*

7. Give a brief chalktalk about helpful and unhelpful responses when a partner's alarm is sounding.

> **When someone close to you sounds an alarm, stop and think.** What do you think is going on inside them during this *emotional*

time. Is this alarm ringing because of past history, old hurts, and vulnerabilities? Is there anything you can do to diminish or turn off the alarm by responding to your partner's call with care, empathy, and reassurance? What actions can you take to provide security and promote trust?

The key to responding to your partner's alarm is listening. This means listening not so much to the words said, but to the feelings conveyed and to the needs and longings beneath the surface. Getting to the heart of the matter is not easy, but this is what is needed. When you can respond on this level, your partner is more likely to feel truly heard and cared about. This builds security and trust that will eventually shut off your partner's alarm.

Your partner's alarms will often set off your own. This is what makes it hard to stay focused on your partner: your own emotions escalate, your own vulnerabilities may get triggered. It takes self-control to ride out the wave of your own emotion and *stay with your partner*, physically and emotionally. If you turn off, tune out, or walk away, you'll be reinforcing whatever feelings of insecurity your partner already had. If you stay put and make an effort to attend to your partner's needs and feelings, you'll probably strengthen the bonds between you.

8. Invite couples to reflect on typical alarm-ringing situations in their relationship.

   Turn your worksheet over and draw a line down the middle. Label one side with your name and one side with your partner's name.

   Based on what you have just learned about your partner's alarm buttons and your own, make a list of situations that would be likely to set off your partner's emotional alarms. Make a separate list of scenarios that would typically trigger your own alarms.

   Try to think of common, everyday examples (teasing, forgetting a commitment, nagging, coming home late, etc.) instead of extreme, explosive situations (having an affair).

9. After 2–3 minutes of individual brainstorming, ask partners to share their lists with one another and choose two scenarios for role play practice.

   Exchange lists with your partner and read them with an open mind. Your goal is to understand the other person's perception of his alarm buttons and yours.

➤ Once you have a joint picture of your different triggers, each person choose one situation when your emotional alarm buttons usually go off. In the next segment, you will role play these alarming situations.

10. When everyone has identified a situation, give instructions and ground rules for the first round of role-playing.

➤ Partners will take turns role-playing the situation you chose. The goal of the role play is for your partner to respond in a way that will turn off or tone down your alarm.

➤ Start with the older person's alarm-ringing role-play situation. You are the **Alarm Ringer.** Pretend that your feared scenario has happened.

➢ Imagine that you are at home with your partner, talking about the event as if it has just happened.

➢ Act out the emotional response you would have to this event. Try to really experience those feelings.

➤ Younger partners are the **Alarm Stoppers.** Try to respond in a way that will turn off your partner's alarm, if possible.

➢ Hold your partner's **Alarm Clock** worksheet on your lap and refer to it as often as needed to keep you focused on unique vulnerabilities of your partner that may be causing him to become so emotional in this situation.

➢ Try to respond in a way that will eliminate your partner's need for any alarm such as offering reassurance, acknowledging his feelings, touching, words of concern, etc.

➤ Role plays will last just 1 minute, a signal will be given to stop the role play.

☞ *Blow your horn or harmonica to demonstrate the sound signal. Invite questions from participants and when you have responded to these, give people the go-ahead to start their role plays, giving the musical cue for folks to begin.*

11. After 1 minute, give the signal to stop and then ask couples to talk about how it went. (2–3 minutes)

➤ **Alarm Ringers,** give *Alarm Stoppers* feedback about what they did that was most helpful to you.

➢ Be specific and descriptive (*you took my hand, looked in my eyes, and told me you were sorry I was upset*).

➢ **Alarm Stoppers,** briefly describe how you felt trying to respond to *Alarm Ringers.*

> **Alarm Ringers,** give *Alarm Stoppers* a specific suggestion as to something they could do differently in the next role play.

12. Give instructions for couples to try the role play a second time.

> Try the role play again, this time with **Alarm Stoppers** using the approach suggested by *Alarm Ringers*.

☞ *Interrupt with your signal after 1 minute. Ask people to process what happened.*

> **Alarm Ringers,** give *Alarm Stoppers* feedback about how well this new approach worked in stopping your alarms.

13. Invite couples to share examples of successful approaches to turning off their partner's alarms. Then instruct everyone to switch roles. The older partner becomes the **Alarm Stopper** and the younger partner uses the **Alarm Ringer** role-play scenario they chose earlier. Repeat *Steps 10–12* with these new role plays. (4–5 minutes)

☞ *Signal when to begin and stop and remind folks to keep their feedback descriptive, specific, and positive, focusing on what helped to turn off alarms, even if it caused only a slight improvement in Alarm Ringer's emotional state.*

14. Solicit feedback again about the kinds of actions that couples found to be helpful in turning off their partner's alarms. Respond to any frustrations expressed by people who felt helpless or ineffective in responding to their partner's feelings and weave these issues into a closing chalktalk about the difficulty and importance of using these skills for maintaining closeness in a relationship.

● **Turning off your partner's alarm is hard work.** In reality, you do not have the actual power to turn off anyone's feelings: only they can do that. But your actions *can* and *do* have a tremendous effect on your partner. Your responses to your partner during an *emotional time* can help maintain closeness or distance; understanding or misunderstanding; forgiveness or resentment; commitment or rejection.

● **Honing your relationship skills takes time and practice.** This is not always going to be a fun time so naturally you might want to avoid putting yourself through the sometimes grueling paces of trying to understand your partner and find solutions to the conflicts or painful issues that will inevitably crop up between you.

But as with any skill or creative endeavor, once you get it, you'll be able to perform the moves with the agility of a seasoned athlete or dancer. Then you'll probably wake up to pleasant music instead of a disturbing alarm.

VARIATIONS

▨ Ask each couple to bring in a small tape cassette player and a tape of their *least favorite* music. In *Step 10,* start the music at a moderate level when they start the role play. Give control of the volume to the **Alarm Ringer,** who turns the volume up when they experience their feelings starting to escalate, and turns the volume down when the actions of their partner are starting to help them feel calmer.

▨ To explore gender differences, insert a fishbowl activity after *Step 8.* Have all the wives gather in a circle and share their typical alarms while husbands observe. Then invite the men to compare notes in the inner circle while their wives watch. Afterwards, pair up in marital couples or other mixed-gender dyads to talk about insights.

▨ After *Step 4,* take a break. Post all worksheets in a gallery and invite couples to stroll the gallery, viewing the differences and similarities in people's emotional alarms. Ask couples if they recognize their partner's **Alarm Clock.**

Background material for this exercise was contributed by Dr. Sue Johnson.

ALARM CLOCK

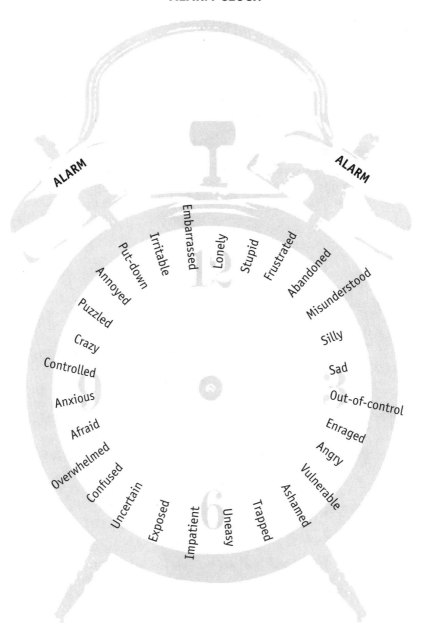

17 STICKS AND STONES

This consciousness-raising exercise helps participants explore the universal potential of violence in relationships and the individual's responsibility to choose nonviolent methods of problem solving.

GOALS

To recognize a wide range of violent behaviors and assess personal use of these behaviors.

To raise consciousness about the negative effects of violence, take responsibility for abusive behavior, and identify nonviolent alternatives for resolving conflict.

GROUP SIZE

Unlimited.

TIME FRAME

50–60 minutes.

MATERIALS NEEDED

Newsprint; marker; **Violent Behavior Inventory** worksheet; resources list of local, state, and national organizations promoting nonviolence or offering services for individuals and families dealing with violence issues.

PROCESS

This process is intended to be a consciousness-raising experience for groups of relatively healthy individuals who are interested in violence as an issue, motivated to explore their own use of violence, and willing to take steps for changing personal behavior.

When preparing resource lists, be sure to include domestic abuse projects, antiviolence groups, support groups in your community, and names of therapists with competencies in violence/abuse issues.

1. Invite participants to share their motivations for coming and use these responses to highlight your agenda, philosophy, and ground rules for participation.

    The end of violence begins with you. The key is to start by exploring your *own* violent behavior rather than the behavior of others.

● **Nearly everyone is violent sometimes.** This does not condone, excuse, or minimize the devastating effects of violence. It simply means that violent behavior occurs on a continuum, from hurtful words to hurtful actions. Most people are violent at some time in their lives—if not with family, then with friends, neighbors, co-workers, strangers, social or political groups, property, or pets. We all need to take responsibility for our own behavior.

● **Admitting personal violence can be painful and scary.** In order to be honest *with yourself,* it is important that you feel safe. You need to know that you can keep your history of violence private, if you wish. Anything you choose to share in this group is confidential—as long as it falls outside child protection laws.

   ▨ *Clarify that child protection laws offer an exception to confidentiality rules. In most states, if a participant tells about a recent act of abuse resulting in harm, or danger of harm, to minor children, facilitators and health professionals are required by law to report these incidents.*

2. Invite participants to give examples of violent or abusive behaviors in a family or intimate relationship. Weave responses into a chalktalk on violence and abusive behaviors.

   ● **Violence is an inappropriate use of power and control** resulting in harm (or threats of harm) to people, property, animals, social groups, community organizations, or environment. Pioneering advocate of nonviolent social change, Mohandas Gandhi, lived by his belief that "Any attempt to impose your will on another person is an act of violence."

   ● **Violence can take many forms,** from physical trauma to stony silence. Shaking your fist in someone's face, calling your child lazy, slashing the tires of your boyfriend's car, shouting at your boss, insulting your wife or husband, kicking out a door, doing nothing when someone else is hurting—all are acts of violence.

   ● **All forms of violence are hurtful.** Although we all learned the childhood chant, *Sticks and stones can break my bones, but words can never hurt me,* we all know that this rhyme is a myth. Words *do* hurt us. *All* forms of violence— verbal, emotional, psychological, physical, and sexual—are hurtful and not okay. A better rhyme to teach our kids would be, *Sticks and stones can break my bones and words can really hurt me.*

3. Invite participants to apply this broader definition of violence to their own behaviors. (4–6 minutes)

> Given this broad definition of violence, jot down examples of when you've engaged in a violent or abusive behavior in the past few days.

>> Remember, using power to try to control someone, or withholding your affection or attention can be abusive just as much as slapping your child or shoving someone out of the way.

>> Try to recall instances of abusive attitudes, tone of voice, comments, action or inaction, and the situations that provoked them.

>> *Prompt with other examples (refusing to kiss your partner good-bye because you were angry, yelling at your son because he didn't finish his homework, slamming the door hard in anger, etc.).*

> Now think back over the past year and recall several other instances when, in retrospect, you can see that you were verbally, emotionally, physically, or sexually abusive.

>> Make note of the provoking situation and your response.

>> Remember, you will not be forced to share any information unless you choose to.

4. Invite volunteers to share a few examples of violent or abusive behavior and the trigger situations. After several people have shared their responses, brainstorm with the group about possible *provocations of violence or abuse,* listing ideas on newsprint. (5–7 minutes)

   The list might look something like this: social/cultural norms and values condoning violence, history of abuse as a child, frustration, anger, stress, alcohol, drugs, lack of skills, lack of alternatives to violence or abuse, loss of control, belief that violence or abuse is necessary, appropriate, or one's right as a man/woman/parent/citizen, etc., personal choice to use power and control to dominate others.

5. Weave responses into a chalktalk on personal responsibility for violence/abuse.

   ● **Violent or abusive behavior is always a personal choice or decision.** External stress and provocation, anger, alcohol and drugs, childhood abuse, and other factors do not *cause* you to behave abusively. You choose violence because you want to make someone else change *their* actions or behavior—to get the kids to be quiet or behave, to stop your partner from leaving you, to get attention from a distant spouse. When you decide to use violence for these reasons, you probably think the end justifies the means. But it never does.

Violence is never okay except for self-defense. Regardless of its prevalence in our society, there is no justification for a choice to engage in acts of violence. It is against the law, causes immeasurable harm, and is unacceptable behavior.

Violence is painful to admit. When we are violent or abusive, we may feel guilty, ashamed, or fearful afterwards. Most people use three defenses to reduce the intensity of feelings about their violence.

Denial: You pretend the violent or abusive behavior never happened.

Minimization: You minimize the seriousness of the violence or its effects.

Blaming: You blame someone or something outside yourself for your violence: stress, alcohol, your temper, our violent society, your parents (who abused you), your partner, your kids, your boss, the economy, the government, the weather, etc.

Stopping violent behavior and remaining violence-free requires commitment. You have to *choose* nonviolent solutions to conflict. A commitment to nonviolence means using healthy alternatives for managing feelings of frustration, anger, fear, hurt, jealousy, and other difficult emotions. This means letting go of control and power, giving up your investment in winning, embracing your humanity, and feeling your pain.

Commitment to nonviolence requires personal action. If you want to stop violent or abusive behaviors, you need to stop first and think about your motivation.

Are you willing to look honestly at your own behavior without denying, minimizing, or blaming others for your actions?

Are you willing to search for alternatives to violence and make a commitment to developing new alternatives to violence?

Nonviolence is a decision, a decision that only you can make.

6. Distribute the **Violent Behavior Inventory** worksheets. Invite those interested in changing violent behavior to start with an honest reflection about the nature and extent of their use of violence. (4–6 minutes)

Read each example of violent behavior and reflect on how often you engage in this behavior.

Put a check mark beside the frequency that best describes your use of this particular form of violence *in the past six months*.

Use the scale at the top of the column.

N = Never, R = Rarely, O = Occasionally, F = Frequently,
VF = Very Frequently.
> Be as honest with yourself as possible and respond to each item.

7. After 6 minutes, interrupt individual reflections and invite folks to share feedback about the violence inventory and to describe some of the feelings that emerged during reflection.

✓ Were you surprised by any of the violent behaviors listed or your response to these items?

8. Challenge the group to shift gears and focus on healthier alternatives to violent or abusive behaviors. Solicit examples of possible nonviolent responses to provocative situations the group has described. Reinforce points made earlier about personal responsibility.

● **Violence is only one of many possible responses to a situation.** We all choose violence, at least occasionally, but it is important to remember that violence is always a *choice*. We always have other options—and we need to be prepared with alternatives, especially at times of high stress.

9. Ask people to personalize the issue by selecting a situation which might tempt them to use violence. Work with a partner to find nonviolent alternatives for handling this situation. (6–8 minutes)

> On the back of your inventory, write a short description of a situation which might tempt you to use violent or abusive behavior.

> This can be a real-life situation or an imaginary one. For ideas, refer back to items on your **Violent Behavior Inventory**.

> Pick a situation that is *moderately difficult* for you to handle; it should not be your most challenging situation.

> *Wait until everyone has identified and written a situation.*

> Pair up with someone you do not know well.

> Decide who will be *Fair* and who will be *Just*.

> *Fairs* go first. Read or describe your situation to your partner. Give your worksheet to your partner and then discuss together possible alternative nonviolent responses to your dilemma.

> In 2 minutes, brainstorm as many nonviolent ideas as you can.

> *Just,* write down all nonviolent alternatives to *Fair's* situation.

> When you hear the signal that 2 minutes are up, switch roles so *Justs* can read or describe your dilemma. Then brainstorm a list of nonviolent alternatives for your situation.

> **Fair,** write down all nonviolent alternatives to *Just's* situation.

> *Signal the group when 2 minutes are up, and it's time to switch roles.*

10. Poll the group on the numbers of nonviolent alternatives they generated. Solicit many examples of nonviolent options and use them to illustrate your closing summary on personal responsibility.

    ● **There is always at least one alternative to violence: nonviolence.** Deciding *not* to be violent opens the door to other alternatives such as compassion, tolerance, compromise, sharing feelings honestly and respectfully, accepting responsibility for your own behavior and feelings, problem-solving, relaxing, exercising, praying, meditating, and many other nonabusive alternatives, including nonviolent social and political action.

11. Lead a closing discussion about positive actions people could take as individuals or collectively to advocate nonviolence in our society. Ask people to make a personal commitment to change at least one violent behavior or advocate nonviolence in society.

    > Write a statement of one action you will take to challenge violence in our society or promote nonviolent methods of resolving conflict.

12. Invite people to share plans for change, then hand out resource lists and briefly discuss local, state, and national resources for addressing violence and abuse issues on a personal or societal level.

VARIATIONS

▨ Expand your session by adding a skill-building component to *Step 8.*

▨ As part of your closing, incorporate a personal challenge and pledge to nonviolence using questions from the chalktalk in *Step 5.*

▨ Contact the Domestic Abuse Intervention Project, 206 W. 4th Street, Duluth Minnesota, 55806, 218-722-2781 for additional training resources, including excellent videos, on the topic of family violence.

Conceptual ideas for this exercise were contributed by Ellen Pence and the Domestic Abuse Intervention Project in Duluth, Minnesota, and can be found in Ellen Pence and Michael Paymar's groundbreaking book, Education Groups for Men Who Batter: The Duluth Model *(New York: Springer Publishing Company, Inc., 1993).*

VIOLENT BEHAVIOR INVENTORY

Place a check mark in the box under the frequency that best describes your use of this particular form of violence *in the past six months*. Use the scale at the top of the column (N = Never, R = Rarely, O = Occasionally, F = Frequently, VF = Very Frequently).

PHYSICAL ABUSE/VIOLENCE

	N	R	O	F	VF
Slapping, hitting, punching, kicking, biting, poking, pulling hair	☐	☐	☐	☐	☐
Pushing, grabbing, shoving, throwing, knocking down	☐	☐	☐	☐	☐
Choking, holding hand over mouth, squeezing throat	☐	☐	☐	☐	☐
Using or threatening to use weapons: guns, knives, etc.	☐	☐	☐	☐	☐
Shaking your fist in someone's face	☐	☐	☐	☐	☐
Walking around like you are about to blow up	☐	☐	☐	☐	☐
Standing in a way that crowds someone or intimidates them	☐	☐	☐	☐	☐
Yelling and screaming, raising your voice in a threatening way	☐	☐	☐	☐	☐
Destroying furniture or other property in your home or in someone else's home	☐	☐	☐	☐	☐
Hurting animals or pets	☐	☐	☐	☐	☐
Spanking a child so hard you leave marks	☐	☐	☐	☐	☐
Chasing someone in your car, trying to run her/him off the road	☐	☐	☐	☐	☐
Forcing someone to do something against his/her will	☐	☐	☐	☐	☐
Restraining someone from leaving a room or moving	☐	☐	☐	☐	☐

EMOTIONAL, PSYCHOLOGICAL, OR VERBAL ABUSE/VIOLENCE

Threatening to harm someone or harm yourself	☐	☐	☐	☐	☐
Grilling someone on her/his behavior, giving the *third degree*	☐	☐	☐	☐	☐
Using sarcasm or an insulting voice	☐	☐	☐	☐	☐
Calling names, putting down someone, putting down their friends	☐	☐	☐	☐	☐
Telling someone she/he is dumb, stupid, fat, ugly, lazy, worthless	☐	☐	☐	☐	☐
Threatening to abandon children	☐	☐	☐	☐	☐
Trying to keep your partner or your children isolated from friends, relatives, activities	☐	☐	☐	☐	☐
Telling your kids lies or derogatory information about their mother or father	☐	☐	☐	☐	☐
Threatening to take the children and disappear	☐	☐	☐	☐	☐
Threatening to sue for custody or never pay child support	☐	☐	☐	☐	☐
Calling your partner an unfit parent, threatening to call protective services as an intimidation tactic	☐	☐	☐	☐	☐
Humiliating someone in front of family or friends	☐	☐	☐	☐	☐
Making someone do something degrading or humiliating	☐	☐	☐	☐	☐
Sabotaging your partner's existing job through harassment	☐	☐	☐	☐	☐
Checking up on partner's activities, listening to his/her phone conversations	☐	☐	☐	☐	☐
Making your partner depend on you for transportation or money	☐	☐	☐	☐	☐
Acting jealous and possessive when your partner is around others	☐	☐	☐	☐	☐
Insisting on making all the major decisions in the family	☐	☐	☐	☐	☐
Controlling all the money, how it gets spent	☐	☐	☐	☐	☐

VIOLENT BEHAVIOR INVENTORY (CONTINUED)

SEXUAL ABUSE/VIOLENCE

	N	R	O	F	VF
Demanding or forcing sex	❏	❏	❏	❏	❏
Making sexually degrading statements about your partner	❏	❏	❏	❏	❏
Committing violent sexual acts	❏	❏	❏	❏	❏
Insisting your partner view pornography against her/his will	❏	❏	❏	❏	❏
Withholding sex and affection as punishment	❏	❏	❏	❏	❏
Assaulting someone's breasts or genitals	❏	❏	❏	❏	❏
Touching or making someone else touch you when he/she does not want to	❏	❏	❏	❏	❏
Making inappropriate sexual statements to children	❏	❏	❏	❏	❏
Making children watch you be sexual with your partner	❏	❏	❏	❏	❏
Exposing your nudity to children as a sexual turn-on	❏	❏	❏	❏	❏
Invading children's privacy during dressing, bathing	❏	❏	❏	❏	❏
Using children for sexual gratification, including fantasy	❏	❏	❏	❏	❏

OTHER ABUSIVE OR VIOLENT BEHAVIORS

	N	R	O	F	VF
Making degrading remarks or jokes about minority groups	❏	❏	❏	❏	❏
Joining a racist group or a militant militia	❏	❏	❏	❏	❏
Attacking gays and lesbians, Jews, or other people who are different from you	❏	❏	❏	❏	❏
Supporting or not challenging racist/sexist/homophobic/ fattist behaviors	❏	❏	❏	❏	❏
Teaching your children to hate certain groups	❏	❏	❏	❏	❏
Expecting women to accept male authority	❏	❏	❏	❏	❏
Threatening to hurt someone, hurt his/her loved ones, or damage her/his property	❏	❏	❏	❏	❏
Watching violent TV programs or movies	❏	❏	❏	❏	❏
Using violent language	❏	❏	❏	❏	❏
Making obscene gestures to people	❏	❏	❏	❏	❏
Shouting and making a scene in public	❏	❏	❏	❏	❏
Defacing public property	❏	❏	❏	❏	❏
Physically assaulting someone	❏	❏	❏	❏	❏
Throwing sticks and stones	❏	❏	❏	❏	❏
Advocating the use of force and violence	❏	❏	❏	❏	❏
Carrying a weapon and using it regularly to threaten people	❏	❏	❏	❏	❏
Shouting insults to athletes, coaches, referees, other parents, or fans at sports events	❏	❏	❏	❏	❏
Forcing someone to commit a crime	❏	❏	❏	❏	❏
Trashing the environment	❏	❏	❏	❏	❏
Playing violent video games or other games involving hurting/killing	❏	❏	❏	❏	❏

18 DIVORCE RECOVERY RITUALS

Participants create personal and family rituals that will aid in recovery from the trauma of divorce.

GOALS

To appreciate the power of rituals to ease difficult life changes and enhance adjustment to divorce.

To identify personal and family problems resulting from divorce and create rituals that aid in recovery from these losses.

GROUP SIZE

Unlimited.

TIME FRAME

60–70 minutes.

MATERIALS NEEDED

Newsprint; marker; blank paper; **Recovery Rituals** worksheet; horn or harmonica for trainer's use; recommended reading and resource list of books, organizations, and groups dealing with divorce issues.

PROCESS

1. Welcome everyone, introduce yourself, and give a brief overview of your agenda. Distribute blank paper and invite participants to reflect on the changes that have disrupted their lives as a part of the divorce process. (2 minutes)

   ➤ As quickly as you can, without stopping to think too long or hard about it, write down a list of all the problems you or your children are having as you recover from divorce.

      ➤ Write whatever comes to mind without censoring or judging your thoughts.

2. Encourage people to add to this problem list during the rest of the exercise, noting that additional problems will occur to them as others share their experience. Then guide participants through a brief icebreaker to get acquainted and warmed up to the topic. (6–8 minutes)

   ➤ Pair up with someone you do not know well, introduce yourself by first name, and tell a little about your family situation (when you were divorced, how long you were married, and if you have children, their names and ages).

☞ *Interrupt after 3 minutes.*

➤ Now tell about various changes you and your family have experienced as a result of divorce (sold your home, moved, went back to work, lived on less money, etc.).

3. After 5–6 minutes, reconvene the group and invite people to share examples of changes they experienced as a result of divorce. Summarize common changes and losses and weave into a short chalktalk about the potentially disruptive nature of divorce. (4–5 minutes)

● **Divorce is a cultural event with varying degrees of stress.** All families experiencing divorce go through a process of disorganization and reorganization. For most people, the first year is the worst, with an overwhelming number of changes occurring in a relatively short period of time.

● **Divorce is a common experience in our culture.** In the United States, over 50 percent of all marriages end in divorce. Approximately 25 percent of households in the United States are headed by solo parents. But no matter how common divorce is, you can feel terribly alone when you go through it.

● **We have no cultural traditions or rituals for divorce.** Despite its prevalence in our society, we have no way to acknowledge the end of a marital relationship apart from signing final divorce papers and paying legal fees. There is no "undoing" ceremony, no grieving ritual, or no healing service. Lack of divorce rituals means you have no formal way to acknowledge your losses and receive support at a painful time of your life.

4. Ask participants to share words that pop into their minds when they hear the word *divorce* and list these on newsprint. (3 minutes)

☞ *Most will be negative: pain, loss, anger, guilt, shame, feelings of failure, embarrassment, disappointment, hurt, revenge, bitterness, escape, etc.*

5. Integrate participant responses into a chalktalk on common myths about divorce.

● **There is no positive context for divorce in our culture.** Divorce is considered bad, in part due to certain myths about divorce.

○ **Myth #1: Divorce breaks up the family.** In reality, divorce is a legal (and emotional) dissolution of a marriage, not a family. Parents are still parents to their children; the parent-child relationship is not ended. What divorce does is create new family configurations, where children, in most cases, are still loved and cared for by both custodial and noncustodial parents.

Myth #2: Divorce is a permanent state rather than a condition subject to change. The majority of divorced people eventually remarry, many within the first three years following divorce.

Myth #3: Family disruption is always a fact in divorce situations. This is not always true. Adults and children vary greatly in the amount of turmoil and trauma experienced because of divorce. Additional stress and adversity may prolong recovery, but most people feel better in six months to two years.

6. Introduce the concept of rituals and their importance in life transitions.

Rituals are a central part of life, a way of using familiar symbols or symbolic actions to ease what would otherwise be unfamiliar life changes. They are a unique way to embrace continuity and change at the same time. For example, wedding rituals—rings, flowers, music, etc.—all bring familiar, reassuring elements to the uncertainty of a new marriage and an unknown future.

Rituals serve multiple purposes: *healing* from loss or hurt, *coping* with life change, *connecting* to self and others, *rebuilding* personal and family life, and *celebrating*. We learn rituals from our ancestors and from social, cultural, and religious groups.

Rituals and traditions are ways of making meaning from your life, from old and new experiences. They can be simple or elaborate, happy, sad, or bittersweet. Some rituals, like a good-night kiss, may be done daily; others, like a baptism, may be done once in a lifetime.

7. Invite participants to compare notes with several different people. (10–12 minutes)

> Stand up and find a partner who you do not know.

> Tell your partner about a ritual or tradition you have learned for *coping with life change*.

- This can be a well-known ritual like marriage or high school graduation or a unique, personal, or family ritual like singing together or making funny home videos.

- You each have 1 minute to share your ritual or tradition.

> *Give a signal when time is up and you want participants to move on to a new partner.*

> Now move on to another person whom you do not know well.

> This time share a ritual you have for *connecting with yourself or others*.

> Perhaps you have rituals for alone time with your children or weekly long-distance calls to a parent, sibling, or friend.

> *After 2 minutes, give the signal to change partners.*

> Find another new partner and now tell about a ritual or tradition that you have for *healing from hurts or loss*.

> This can be a simple ritual, like letting yourself have a good cry, or an elaborate ritual, like a funeral or a good-bye party.

> *After 2 minutes, give the signal to change partners.*

> Say good-bye to this partner and move on to another partner.

> Now share a ritual you have used for *rebuilding your life or family*.

> Remodeling your home, family meetings, new rules or limits are examples of rebuilding rituals you might have used to create order and organization in your life.

> *After 2 minutes, give the signal to change partners.*

> Bid farewell to your partner and find another new partner.

> Share an example of a ritual you have used for *celebrating life or people*.

> Birthday parties, family stories, special meals, flowers, champagne, and prayers are some rituals you might have used for celebrating and affirming people or events.

8. Reconvene the group and invite people to share examples of each type of ritual. Hand out the **Recovery Rituals** worksheets and encourage people to take notes in the left column as you briefly discuss the purpose of each ritual and give examples relevant to recovery from divorce. (6–8 minutes)

   ● **Life change rituals** are designed to help us deal with a change of role or status such as changing from married to single, housewife to employee, parent to grandparent. Using your maiden name after divorce, taking off your wedding ring, and forwarding your ex-partner's mail are all rituals symbolic of your new marital status.

   ● **Healing rituals** are rituals that help us or others heal from hurts, physical, emotional, and spiritual. This includes finding ways to let go, give and receive comfort, seek and grant forgiveness, express feelings, lick your wounds, and be tender with yourself and others. In divorce, this means finding a way to honor the importance of your past marriage and eventually let it go. Children need extra love and attention at these times and opportunities to express feelings like sadness, anger, and fear.

Connecting rituals. Meditation, prayer, long walks in the woods, annual spiritual retreats away from family, and journaling are rituals that might help you connect to yourself and your values. Visits with family, lunch with friends, and annual community projects are rituals which could provide important links to others.

During divorce, connections with others provide needed continuity and meaning at a time of loss. For children, staying connected to both parents, grandparents, and extended family is very important.

Rebuilding rituals. Divorce can feel like an earthquake, shaking up the very foundation of your life and family. You feel like your world is topsy-turvy. Kids often express their feelings in actions, sometimes by misbehaving at home or at school. Rebuilding rituals restore order: family meetings, new limits, bedtime stories, new furniture, new chores for children, etc.

Celebrating rituals. Even when things are bad, you can find reasons to celebrate life and love, affirm yourself and others for strengths and achievements, and restore joy, humor, and laughter in your heart and home. Divorce is a time when celebrating rituals are a need (a pie breakfast with your friends on Thanksgiving Day or movie and popcorn parties on Friday evenings).

9. Announce that participants will have the opportunity to create rituals that might aid in recovery from divorce. Ask them to take a minute to update the problem list they made at the beginning of the exercise with additional issues that have surfaced during discussion.

10. Allow a minute or two and then ask participants to reflect on which type of ritual would be most suited to the type of problems they are having. (4–5 minutes)

➤ Transfer the problems from your list onto the center column of your **Recovery Rituals** worksheet, matching each problem with one of the five rituals that you think would be most appropriate or helpful for responding to this problem or situation.

☞ *Allow a few minutes for matching problems with rituals.*

> Now look over your entire problem list and pick one for which you would like to create a new recovery ritual.

> *Circle* the problem that you have chosen to focus on.

11. Invite people to work in small teams to create rituals that would assist them in recovery from divorce. (12–15 minutes)

> Join two other participants and form a triad.

> Take turns sharing your chosen problem and the ritual category you paired with this problem. Then, as a team, brainstorm possible rituals that would be meaningful and helpful to each of you in dealing with your problem.

> You each have 4 minutes of group time to receive help from teammates in brainstorming possible rituals.

> When you hear the time signal, shift your focus to the next person and work on helping this person create a new ritual.

> You do not have to agree to your team's suggestions; just stay open to ideas and decide for yourself what ritual you want to try, if any.

> On your worksheet, in the column for rituals, write notes about your favorite ritual ideas beside the appropriate ritual/problem category.

Interrupt every 3–4 minutes with a signal.

12. Reconvene the group and invite people to share examples of rituals they created with the help of their team. Respond to questions or comments about what folks have learned, then refer people who want to learn more about rituals to Janine Roberts and Ivan Ember Black's classic book, *Rituals for Changing Times* (New York: HarperPerennial, 1992). Hand out the recommend reading and resource list of books, organizations, and local groups dealing with divorce issues.

13. Close the meeting with a favorite ritual of your own (group hug, affirmations, resolution statements, standing ovation, etc.).

VARIATION

▣ Divide the group into five small groups, one for each of the five ritual categories. Assign each group the task of creating a ritual that would promote healing or recovery in their assigned area. Have each group create a short skit or demonstration of their new ritual.

RECOVERY RITUALS

COMMON RITUALS	PROBLEMS	NEW RITUALS
Life change rituals		
Healing rituals		
Connecting rituals		
Rebuilding rituals		
Celebrating rituals		

19 COPING WITH FAMILY STRESS

This fascinating exercise allows participants to watch what happens when a stressed family adopts the beliefs and behaviors of families who have been successful in coping with stress.

GOALS

To identify five key beliefs and five important behaviors of families who cope well with stress.

To raise awareness of how family stress is different from other stress and how change in one family member's style of coping with stress affects everyone in the family.

To apply effective coping skills to current family stress.

GROUP SIZE

Unlimited.

TIME FRAME

45–60 minutes.

MATERIALS NEEDED

Newsprint; marker; ten (3"x5") cards, each labeled with one of five beliefs and five behaviors (described in *Step 5*), along with an example of each; **Coping with Family Stress** worksheet.

PROCESS

1. Invite people to brainstorm a list of events or circumstances, both inside and outside their family, that contribute to chronic family stress. List all ideas on newsprint.

    Come prepared with your own list of examples for prompting reflection by participants (chronic illness or disability, death of a family member, financial difficulties, behavior problems with children, legal problems, divorce, single parenting, remarriage/stepfamily, new baby, etc.).

2. Summarize stressors participants have in common and weave these examples into a chalktalk about family stress. (5–10 minutes)

    ● **Family stress exists when family life gets out of control.** What used to be manageable becomes unmanageable: you can't pay your bills, control your rebellious teenager, clean the house, function on your job, sleep at night, or get along with your partner. Tension in your family builds; kids squabble about everything; nothing gets done; you feel strung-out, guilty, and desperate for time away.

Family stress is different from other forms of stress because of the interrelationships involved. If one member of your family is under stress, it affects the entire family. Having a severely ill child means parents may miss work to provide intensive child care while other children must cope with less attention from parents, take on more responsibilities at home, or spend more time in day care. Everyone feels the stress.

Stress originates both inside and outside your family. Expecting yourself to be a perfect parent can create stress, so can conflict between siblings or differing values of husband and wife. But stress can also come from outside when dad gets transferred or loses his job, or mom has to work rotating shifts. Internal stress is created by your own expectations, attitudes, or behaviors, whereas external stress (like war, poverty, or racism) is caused by external events not under your control. Both can have a powerful effect on you and your family.

While some stress is good, continually living at your peak is unhealthy. We all need some stress; the only people without stress are dead people. Stress is part of staying busy, living a stimulating life, and being energized to set goals, meet deadlines, and finish what you start. But when stress remains at a high peak for too long, family members can develop symptoms or become ill: get depressed, abuse alcohol or drugs, act out in school, develop an ulcer.

Families differ in abilities to cope with severe stress. Some families have a very hard time. They give up, give in, or simply can't get a handle on it. The stress takes over and, in essence, runs their lives. This creates the *out of control* quality that highly stressed families experience. But other families manage to live through periods of extreme stress—raising a handicapped or disabled child, caring for terminally ill relatives, living through job loss—and still *function normally* or even *thrive*. Why is this?

Families who cope well with stress think and behave differently from those who do not fare so well. Effective stress handlers expect stress as a normal, sometimes even positive, part of life. These beliefs underscore their actions, which are solution-focused. Setting new priorities for time and sharing responsibilities in a different way are typical behaviors of families who successfully cope with stress.

3. Announce that participants will have an opportunity to figure out a puzzle: identify beliefs and behaviors of families who cope effectively with stress. Explain that this will involve a role-play demonstration of a stressed family and then ask five people to volunteer for this role play.

4. When five people have agreed to role-play the family, give the volunteers a copy of the role-play scenario. Read it aloud to the entire group and give instructions for deciding on roles.

> *You are a recently divorced family of five. The mother is thirty-nine years old. She is unemployed, receives AFDC and Medical Assistance, goes to business school two days a week, lives with her three children and her sixty-three-year-old disabled mother in a low-income housing project. Grandmother is an insulin-dependent diabetic who needs a kidney transplant. The oldest son, fifteen years old, is a gifted student who excels in music. The second child, a daughter ten years old, likes sports but has a foot deformity and also needs an operation. The youngest son, aged eight years, misses his father, who moved out of state last year.*

> Take 30 seconds to choose which role you want to play in the family scenario and then come take a seat up front.

>> *While the family is discussing roles, arrange five chairs for them in a semicircle facing the audience. Encourage the audience to "listen in" on the decision-making process as a clue to unfolding family dynamics.*

5. When the volunteer family has decided on roles, explain the process further to all participants, demonstrating as needed to clarify.

> First, the family will start to interact naturally, pretending you are at home, have just received news that Grandma is next on the list for a kidney transplant, and you are talking about how you will manage this stress.

> After a few minutes, one of the people in the family will be given a 3"x5" card with a key belief of families who cope effectively with stress.

>> When a family member receives a belief card, you should read the belief silently *without revealing it to other family members* and simply adopt your new belief in the family discussion, allowing it to change your verbal comments or behavior.

>> Your goal is to act as if you totally embraced this new belief, but to do it in a subtle way, without actually coming out and telling your family (and observers in the audience) exactly what it is.

© 1997 Whole Person Associates 210 W Michigan Duluth, MN 55802   (800) 247-6789

➤ Observers in the audience will try to guess what new beliefs the person has added.

    ➤ When the chosen family member has had a few minutes to act out the new belief, the role play will be stopped, and you will have an opportunity to guess the belief.

    ➤ After the audience has tried to guess the new belief, the family member who acted out the belief will read the belief card aloud.

    ➤ The whole group will briefly process how the new belief affected the individual adopting it and other members of the family.

➤ Once the belief has been identified and its effects on individuals or the entire family has been briefly discussed, the role play will resume with that person continuing to act out the new belief, while a second person is given another new belief to act out in the family.

➤ After the second family member has had a few minutes to act out the new belief, we will again stop and asks people in the audience to guess this new belief.

➤ We will repeat this process ten times: five times to introduce stress-effective beliefs and five times to experiment with stress-effective behaviors. A short discussion will follow identification of each belief and behavior, to explore effects of these beliefs and behaviors on individuals, and the family's ability to cope with stress.

6. Ask the volunteer family to start the role play. After 1–2 minutes, give someone the first belief card and allow the role play to continue a few more minutes before stopping and inviting observers to guess the new belief. Lead a short discussion about the effects of this belief on the family's ability to cope with stress, then move on to the next role play. Repeat this process until all five beliefs and all five behaviors have been incorporated into the family role play.

    Anyone in the family, regardless of age, can adopt healthy beliefs and behaviors, so give cards out randomly. The role play will demonstrate the point that change in one person, even a child, can, and will, affect the entire family.

7. When role plays are finished, thank volunteers for their participation and lead a discussion about the effects on the family of adopting stress-effective beliefs and behaviors. Then summarize these beliefs and behaviors in a short chalktalk.

    ● **Families who cope effectively with stress have five key beliefs.**

       ○ **Balanced perspective/faith.** Families who cope well with stress have positive beliefs which offset worries or fears (such as faith in God or a higher power). These beliefs help them to see the good side of life and trust that everything will work out.

Normal relationships. It's reassuring to know that no matter how bad things get, some things never change, some relationships continue. You keep attending your Al-Anon support group, you remain on your bowling team, you go to parent-teacher conferences. These normal relationships provide order and continuity in an otherwise chaotic life.

Individual development. Focusing on the individual interests and abilities of each family member can be a wonderful way to reduce stress and experience the satisfaction of seeing someone (who might be yourself!) grow, in spite of internal and external stress. You finish college, your son gets his driver's license, your husband masters the skill of ski-skating—all achievements which provide an opportunity for celebration and family pride.

Positive outlook. Finding the silver lining in your cloud of stress will immediately lower your stress. What helps is discovering the learning or growth that comes from change, even unpleasant or painful change.

Confidence in caregivers. Families who successfully cope with stress believe that people outside the family can help as long as they participate in the process. Confiding in your family doctor, minister, therapist, and other helpers can make a world of difference, especially when you *believe* that it will.

Families who are effective coping with stress have five key behaviors.

Talking to someone about feelings. Instead of holding feelings in or trying to hide them, find people you can talk to about your feelings. This is a critical skill for coping with chronic stress as well as everyday struggles.

Pamper yourself. Give yourself the care and consideration you deserve. Play that round of golf you've been itching to play. Go to bed early with a novel you've been dying to read or treat yourself to lunch with a friend you've been longing to see. Pampering means giving yourself something pleasant when you need it the most.

Put effort into your work at home and at the office. Intentional hard work can offer surprising relief for stress: cleaning

© 1997 Whole Person Associates 210 W Michigan Duluth, MN 55802   (800) 247-6789

a closet, finishing a report, weeding the garden, writing job resumes, and studying for school can help you direct and focus your energy and experience feelings of increased self-esteem, pride, control, and accomplishment.

○ **Put on your thinking cap and study your situation.** Work to understand what's happening to you and your family. Go to the library and check out books on diabetes, join a stepfamilies support group, talk to other people who have experienced bankruptcy. The more you understand your stress, the better you'll be able to cope with it.

○ **Learn to manage your special needs.** If you need a wheelchair ramp for your home, explore resources for building this important accessory. If your partner needs help coping with chronic pain, check out biofeedback programs in your community. Assume that *your needs are important and worth caring for*, no matter how challenging or inconvenient.

8. Distribute the **Coping with Family Stress** worksheets and invite people to apply these ten beliefs and behaviors to their own unique family stress. (5–6 minutes)

➤ Read each sentence stem and reflect on specific beliefs and behaviors which would help you cope with family stress.

➤ Try to think of beliefs and behaviors that fit with your values and lifestyle and are realistic and reasonable for your current life situation (I can pamper myself with a hot bath and good novel, but I can't afford a trip to Hawaii).

➤ Write your ideas and reflections in the space below each item.

9. Invite people to share plans for coping with family stress and then conclude the session by encouraging everyone to give their plan a try.

VARIATION

▦ For a short program, drop the role play in *Steps 3–6* and use only chalktalks followed by reflection on the worksheet.

Content material for this exercise was contributed by Barbara Elliott, PhD. and adapted from her 1983 doctoral research at the University of Minnesota where she studied how families manage chronic stress.

COPING WITH FAMILY STRESS

BELIEFS

1. A belief that helps (or could help) me maintain a balanced perspective is:

2. The relationships that I want to keep normal through this time of stress are:

3. The special interests and talents of family members that I want to keep supporting are:

4. One good thing that has come out of this stressful experience is:

5. The caregivers I know I can trust to help me and my family (if we participate) are:

BEHAVIORS

6. The person(s) I can talk to about my feelings is/are:

7. My favorite way of pampering myself is:

8. The work (home and/or office) that gives me the most pride and satisfaction is:

9. In order to cope better with my stress, I need to learn more about:

10. I need to learn how to manage the following special needs:

20 FREEDOM TO FORGIVE

In this simple, yet profound, exercise, people can experience the peace and freedom that follows an act of true forgiveness.

GOALS

To forgive someone for an offense.

To let go of bitterness, resentment, and anger.

GROUP SIZE

Unlimited.

TIME FRAME

45–60 minutes.

MATERIALS NEEDED

Forgiveness worksheet.

PROCESS

This is a sensitive issue which will probably evoke strong emotions for some people. Come prepared with a referral resource list of professional counselors, clergy and chaplains, and other caregivers in your community. Distribute this handout during or after the session.

1. Begin by giving an overview of the nature and purpose of this exercise on forgiveness. Make sure people understand that participation is voluntary and review ground rules about confidentiality.

   ➤ While you are free to share with people outside the group whatever you want of your own experiences, **all personal information about others in this group is to be kept strictly confidential.**

2. Give a brief chalktalk on eight principles about forgiveness, encouraging people to reflect on the relevance of these principles to their own forgiveness dilemmas.

   ● **Forgiveness is a decision,** an act of your will. When you forgive someone, you make a conscious choice to excuse someone for an offense or fault. The decision need not take a long period of time, but instead can be made on any day you choose. The act of forgiving someone is a decision only you can make.

- **Forgiveness involves letting go of bitterness, resentment, and anger.** Forgiveness means wiping the slate clean, giving up your investment in holding a grudge or staying mad about past hurts.

- **You can decide to forgive anytime.** You need not wait until you're *emotionally ready* to forgive. The act of forgiveness can bring positive emotional changes, especially a sense of peace and freedom.

- **Forgiveness can be granted even though the offender has not sought forgiveness.** You don't have to wait for people to show remorse, apologize, or ask for forgiveness. You can forgive whenever you want, for your own health, well-being, peace of mind, peace with others, and for believers, peace with God.

- **Not forgiving is destructive.** It causes internal conflict and uses a lot of emotional energy that could be focused on more constructive tasks. It also interferes with possible reconciliation.

- **Hurt feelings can be separated from anger and resentment.** If you have been betrayed by someone you trusted, you probably felt both hurt and anger. Emotional pain from a relationship wound can take a long time to heal, like a broken arm that needs a period of time to mend. But anger can be resolved and the person forgiven at any point in the process.

- **Forgiving does not mean forgetting**—but don't let recurring anger consume you. If you have forgiven someone, but the emotion of anger arises afterwards, you can release this anger using internal self-talk to calm down, remind yourself to forgive and let go of anger, and restore the sense of peace you may have had earlier (*Take it easy, my friend. This issue is over, you've dealt with it, don't let yourself get mad all over again,* etc.).

- **Forgiveness is not a sanction for the offender to repeat the offense.** Forgiveness does not mean that you leave yourself open for future offenses. You can forgive someone but still be cautious— or even end the relationship with them. For example, suppose you are engaged and your fiancee is unfaithful to you. You might decide to forgive your fiancee and still cancel the wedding. In other words, your decision to forgive is independent of your decision to continue the engagement.

3. Invite questions or concerns about forgiveness principles. After responding to issues raised, announce that participants will have an opportunity to explore the effects of an offense they have experienced and decide if they want to forgive the person who offended them.

4. Ask participants to select a partner for sharing and support as they reflect on the forgiveness dynamic.

➤ Pair up with someone you do not know well.

➤ Introduce yourself to your partner and briefly share your reactions to the issue of forgiveness.

  ➢ You each have 1 minute to share whatever you want about your responses to the topic.

    ☞ *This is a good time to remind people of their commitment to keep all information about their partner confidential.*

5. After pairs have gotten acquainted, distribute the **Forgiveness** worksheets. Invite participants to reflect on their personal need to forgive as you guide them through the process.

➤ Think over the past few days (months/years/course of your lifetime). Identify a situation where the actions or words of someone else were hurtful to you.

  ➢ In the space for **offense**, write a brief description of what was done (or not done) that caused you pain.

  ➢ Use specific, behavioral descriptions of what happened (*my son swore at me and ran away from home, my friend betrayed a confidence and told one of my secrets to people at the office, my husband called me fat,* etc.).

➤ What **suffering** did this offense cause you?

  ➢ Write examples of problems that resulted from the offense (*I lost my confidence or ability to trust the opposite sex, I didn't sleep well for months, I was unable to concentrate at work*).

➤ What **feelings** did you experience because of this offense?

  ➢ Write down all of the feelings you experienced because of this offense (anger, hurt, resentment, sadness, etc.).

➤ Are you willing to **forgive** today?

    ☞ *Point out that this is a decision, whatever they choose, yes or no.*

  ➢ Record your decision by marking *yes* or *no* on your worksheet.

6. Affirm everyone for taking risks in making a decision, yes or no, about whether to forgive the offense. Invite partners to compare notes.

➤ Whether you decided *yes*, you want to forgive this offense, or *no*, you're not ready to forgive, tell your partner about your decision.

> Take 2 minutes each to describe the offense and whatever you want to share about your suffering and feelings.

> Then tell you partner about your decision to forgive or not.

> Partners who are in the listener role: listen with an empathic ear.

> *Do not give advice or opinions.* Simply listen. Provide acceptance and support by allowing your partner the opportunity to speak without interruptions.

7. Announce when it's time to switch roles. After 4–5 minutes, invite people to formalize and validate their forgiveness decision.

> Complete and sign the **Forgiveness Statement** at the bottom of your worksheet, indicating whether you have or have not forgiven the offense and the offender.

> This will help formalize and validate your forgiveness decision.

> You may want to make some notes on the back of the worksheet about your reasons for this decision right now.

> Take turns reading and signing the statement with your partner, who becomes a supportive witness of your forgiveness decision.

8. Invite participants to share responses to the exercise and raise any final questions they might have. Briefly summarize and review the principles of forgiveness and encourage people to exercise their power to forgive.

● **Decide to forgive and seek forgiveness often**. People are imperfect and make mistakes, sometimes enormous mistakes. Forgiving others and seeking forgiveness for your own offenses produces healthier lives and relationships.

● **Whenever you decide *not* to forgive, revisit this decision** periodically to consider the issue and your attitude again. Forgiveness is a healing gesture.

☞ *As a final wrap-up, remind people of referral resource lists, offer to stay around for 5–10 minutes after the session ends and respond to questions or facilitate referrals if requested.*

VARIATION

▨ Ask a volunteer to record their reflections on the worksheet ahead of time and demonstrate the forgiveness exercise (with the trainer role-playing a partner) prior to dividing into small groups in *Step 4*.

This exercise was contributed by Frederick A. DiBlasio, PhD.

FORGIVENESS

The offense:

My suffering (problems resulting from the offense):

My feelings (including anger, resentment, etc.)

Are you willing to forgive today? (This is a decision) Yes _____ No _____

FORGIVENESS STATEMENT

I, _____ ,
                                      name

(have/have not) forgiven _____
                                         name(s)

for the offense stated above.

Signed: _____   Date: _____

family & work

21 BALANCING WORK AND FAMILY

The sometimes overwhelming stress of balancing work and family is addressed as participants consider common problems and explore strategies that nourish the self as they enhance the quality of life.

GOALS

To explore levels of stress associated with six common problems of balancing work and family.

To identify effective strategies for coping with stress.

To restore balance and enhance the quality of life.

GROUP SIZE

Unlimited.

TIME FRAME

45–60 minutes.

MATERIALS NEEDED

Newsprint; marker; **Balancing Work and Family** worksheet; baskets filled with spirit words (one per page) written on small sheets of paper.

> ☞ *Possible spirit words include: patience, solitude, flexibility, tenderness, creativity, gratitude, relaxation, simplicity, compassion, forgiveness, beauty, humility, assertiveness, understanding, spontaneity, delight, excitement, connection, integrity, playfulness, release, serenity, service, peace, abundance, romance, gentleness, honesty, joy, trust, fun, silence, truth, love, balance.*

PROCESS

1. Begin with a chalktalk describing stresses faced by contemporary families, relabeling participants as pioneers charting new pathways in a changing world.

   * **We are pioneers.** We are trailblazers in unknown territory, moving through a world that is very different from that of our parents and grandparents, especially in terms of expectations for men and women.

   * **The majority of parents work outside the home** for at least some portion of their children's lives. Many parents feel like they have

two full-time jobs and that their work is never done, even though we are supposedly living in an age of leisure with more conveniences, labor saving devices, and disposable income for pleasure. In actuality, we are working more hours than our parents and earning comparatively less.

Roles of mother/father, husband/wife have changed. In today's world, men can win the Pillsbury Bake-Off and women can fly a F-15 fighter jet; gay and lesbian couples may marry in some states and parent children; single parents, divorced, and remarried families are becoming the norm. As the face of the family becomes more diverse, roles become less gender specific. Our roles need to be redefined in the face of these changes.

There is no guidebook for living through these changes. Many of us are making it up as we go, doing the best we can. It is imperative that we find healthy solutions and strategies for resolving these dilemmas and that we support each other in our efforts to create a healthy balance between the demands of home and the office.

2. Ask participants to share examples of ways they experience stress trying to balance work, family, and self-care. List these ideas on newsprint.

3. Distribute the **Balancing Work and Family** worksheets and invite people to reflect on personal stress levels associated with six common stresses of balancing work and family. Personalize your presentation by incorporating examples generated in *Step 2* to illustrate each point.

Never enough time. There are never enough hours in the day to accomplish everything on our agendas. Meanwhile, children are growing up needing us as parents in different ways and at unpredictable times. Often we feel like we are robbing Peter to pay Paul and not giving any area of our lives its full due. The push and pull between work and home, school and church, friends and family, and gardening and housecleaning can leave you so exhausted that all you can do is fall into bed late at night again.

➤ To what degree are you stressed by a lack of time?

➣ Check the box that best describes the frequency with which you experience stress about time: often, sometimes, or seldom.

Difficulty scheduling. Each parent's work schedule, plus each child's school and activity schedule, plus fitting in quality family time and necessary personal time makes for full calendars which can sometimes be overwhelming and stressful. We're grateful for days when just the routine needs to be followed with no extras thrown in—or better yet, vacation days when we can take a well deserved breather.

> How often are you stressed by scheduling difficulties?

> Check the box that describes how often scheduling difficulties create stress in your life.

● **Superman and superwoman myth.** If you buy into this myth, you are trying to do two or three full-time jobs 100 percent perfectly while the needs of your family increase.

An obnoxious ad shows a beautiful, size 3 woman in a red linen suit breezing in from her day at the office with her briefcase in one hand and the groceries and the baby in the other arm. She starts dinner, feeds the family, and then is later shown in a slinky negligee singing *I can bring home the bacon, fry it up in a pan, and when the lights are low, I am all yours baby, ah uh.* This is one example of the superwoman myth that drives some women to expect perfection in themselves, resulting in lowered self-esteem, feelings of failure, irritability, and a host of stress related dis-ease.

Or consider supermen who knock themselves out working long hours, trying to please employers who are trying to squeeze more and more out of a dwindling labor pool. Then they are expected to come home and relate meaningfully to their spouse and kids and share in the household tasks. Not to mention staying in shape to run a marathon. The superman myth can drive some men to distraction and dis-ease as well.

> Do you find yourself trying to live up to the superman or super-woman myth?

> Mark the box that best describes how often you are stressed by perfectionist expectations of yourself.

● **Guilt.** As mothers and fathers, we often feel enormous guilt be-cause we don't think we're spending enough time with our chil-dren, who we feel need more of us than we can give. We feel guilty that we aren't giving our all at the office, while at the same time we are bombarded with pleas from school, church, and community to volunteer our time. Not to mention aging parents who would appreciate our attention. And of course there are lots of opportu-nities to feel guilty because you've neglected your health and fitness by giving up your exercise routine to fit in time to do laundry and buy groceries.

> How often are you stressed by guilt?

  - Record your response in the box that best describes how often you are stressed by guilt.

- **No role models.** We used to be clear about what was woman's work and what was man's work. Now everything is up for grabs and negotiable. It is important to have some tasks you know you're responsible for so you can have a sense of completion and control.

> Does a lack of clarity about your role add to your stress?

  - Mark the box that best describes how often role ambiguity creates stress for you.

- **Isolation.** One of the effects of trying to manage so much is that we may withdraw from friends, cut out social time to fit in another errand, withdraw from professional associations, give up other pursuits and interests which we found pleasurable and nourishing to fit in more work or more time with family. We stop going out to lunch or having friends over for dinner.

  In this isolation we are tempted to turn to partners to be our main and perhaps our only support: best buddy, playmate, lover, coparent, counselor. These expectations are too high, set us up for disappointment, and put additional strain on an already stressed relationship.

> Have your efforts to balance work and family led to isolation?

  - Mark the box that best describes how often you feel isolated.

4. Ask participants to brainstorm successful strategies for coping with the stress of balancing work and family. List ideas on newsprint, affirming strengths and resources of participants.

5. Guide participants through a chalktalk reflecting on potential coping strategies, using the second section of the worksheet. Where possible, incorporate examples generated in *Step 4* as illustrations.

- **Reprioritize** and keep reprioritizing what's really most important to you at this time in your life. Think about your work life and family life in terms of sequencing. When the children are younger, you can do this, and as the children get older, you can do another piece (go back to school, work for a bigger promotion, agree to take more jobs on the road). It involves saying no to some things, planning and recognizing trade-offs, and realizing you have a whole lifetime in which to fit it all in.

> How often do you reprioritize your life?

> Mark the box that best describes how often you use this skill.

Simplify. Eliminate the unnecessary. Use organizing techniques like buying different colored underwear and socks for each child or giving each family member a basket for collecting odds and ends left around the house.

> How often do you try to simplify and organize your family tasks?

> Mark the box that represents the degree to which you use this skill for reducing stress.

Share the load. Young children can pick up toys; teenagers can cook a pot of chili or do a load of laundry; partners can share household tasks. While supervising and following-up on children's tasks can be a chore in itself, and negotiating with partners can be difficult, it's well worth the battle to clarify expectations and share the load.

Don't forget to ask for help outside your family. Older generations had relatives, neighbors, and friends, young and old, to help raise the barn. You too can reach out: have painting parties, join a support group, and share responsibilities with a work team.

> How often do you share your load?

> Mark the box that best describes how often you use this skill.

Replenish. Develop ways to nourish yourself: body, mind, and soul.

Replenish your body. Nourish your body with good food, rest, and good release through exercise, movement, play, meditation, sex, and lots of fun. Taking several breaks during the day just to breathe deeply (into your abdomen) will bring immediate replenishment. Shake off the stress of your day before going home by taking a few minutes to relax, listen to some music, or take off on a guided visualization. This will create a wonderful buffer between work and home.

Build in regular playful release with family members: family pillow fights, bowling with bumper guards even for the adults, family sculpting with Play-doh or clay, food fights or napkin battles—silly no-one-gets-hurt fun.

> How often do you replenish your body?

> Record your reflections on your worksheet.

Replenish your mind. Develop something you can feel passionate about, something that totally consumes you and takes your mind off anything else, an interest that feeds you and fills you and lets the overflow spill love and goodness back to the ones you love. It may be singing or playing piano or listening to jazz or opera or painting or decorating or getting your pilot's license or writing or learning a new language.

> How often do you replenish your mind?

> Mark your responses on your worksheet.

Replenish your soul. Attend worship. Read inspirational books. Take time to be alone: enjoy a walk in the woods, a bike ride on the trail, or a walk in the neighborhood. Ground yourself with Mother Earth and pull strength from the trees and birds. Let yourself just *be*, meditating, reflecting, praying, renewing your spirit.

> How often to you take time to be alone and nourish your soul?

> Record your responses on your worksheet.

Reconnect. Create rituals to reconnect with yourself, your family, your task at hand, and your spiritual source or higher power. Simple rituals such as lighting a candle, inviting a moment of silence, holding hands around the dinner table, having special talk time with each child, sharing stories, songs, and bedtime lullabies can create meaningful, precious connections.

In your work setting, rituals can allow you to focus more clearly on what you're doing and how you are with your team. For example, a ritual weekly lunch with coworkers can solidify work bonds and build supportive connections.

> Do you have rituals or routine activities that help you to reconnect with yourself, your family, friends, and coworkers as well as your spirit?

> Mark the box that best describes the amount of time you use rituals to reconnect with yourself and others?

6. Invite participants to reflect on the overall balance between their level of stress and their use of strategies for coping with this stress.

> Now look back over your worksheet and compare the level of stress you are experiencing with the variety and frequency of coping strategies you use to offset this stress.

> Do you notice any patterns, problems, or areas needing change?

> Write reflections about your overall balance between work, family, and self-care.

7. Encourage everyone to decide on a specific course of action they want to take to restore or maintain balance between work, family, and self-care.

> Look over your worksheet one more time, this time circling one stress problem that you want to focus on over the next month and one skill strategy that you will use to cope with this problem.

8. Invite people to share their plans for restoring or maintaining balance between work and family. Then distribute baskets filled with spirit words and ask everyone to randomly select one or two.

> Pass the basket around the group, taking one or two of the folded slips of paper from the basket before passing it to the next person.

> Open your paper and read the word written on it. This is your spirit word.

> Reflect on your word and see how your word might guide you to find ways to bring balance into your life or enhance the quality of your life right now.

> Periodically during the week, take the word out, take a deep breath, and reflect on its meaning.

> *Caution people that the message of the word may not be immediately apparent when they open it. Tell them it's like a Chinese fortune cookie, and its message or meaning may be different from day to day, depending on personal needs at different times and circumstances.*

9. Close by playing a recording of a favorite lullaby or song which offers words of inspiration, comfort, and care.

Contributed by Sally Strosahl.

BALANCING WORK AND FAMILY

	Frequency of occurrence		
	Often	Sometimes	Seldom
Problems			
Never enough time	❏	❏	❏
Difficulty scheduling	❏	❏	❏
Superman/Superwoman	❏	❏	❏
Guilt	❏	❏	❏
No role models	❏	❏	❏
Isolation	❏	❏	❏
Skills/Solutions			
Repriortize	❏	❏	❏
Simplify	❏	❏	❏
Share the load	❏	❏	❏
Replenish	❏	❏	❏
Body	❏	❏	❏
Mind	❏	❏	❏
Spirit	❏	❏	❏
Reconnect	❏	❏	❏

Reflections/Resolutions:

22 GENDER, MONEY, AND POWER

Participants uncover the meanings of money, gender, and power in their family of origin, current family, and work relationships and use their insights for problem-solving in these areas.

GOALS

To become sensitized to the meanings of gender, money, and power in family of origin, current family, and work relationships.

To make such meanings more explicit and use them as a beginning framework for problem-solving in work and family relationships.

GROUP SIZE

Unlimited.

TIME FRAME

50–60 minutes.

MATERIALS NEEDED

Attitudes toward Money checklist and **Current Marital/Family Issues** worksheets for all; two copies of the **Gender, Money, and Power Issues** questionnaire for each participant.

PROCESS

1. Provide some thought-provoking questions as a warm-up to the topic, inviting a few people to share their responses with the large group.

   ✔ Which topic is more uncomfortable for you to discuss with friends, business associates, partner, and family of origin: money or sex?

   ✔ If I asked each of you to entrust your wallet or purse to an unrelated person sitting next to you for the next hour, how would you feel? Would it be a different feeling if that person were a man or if that person were a woman?

   ✔ If you won the lottery tomorrow, how would that change your life? Would it improve your relationship with your partner? family of origin? friends? Or would it be problematic in any of these relationships?

2. Use participant responses as a lead in to a chalktalk on some of the

hidden meanings of gender, money, and power in cultural, work, and family contexts in our society.

- **Money is not just currency.** Money is a form of energy, the moving force of our civilization. Money does not just allow us to buy material things. Money can also buy us other good things in life: education, health, beauty, entertainment, love, and justice. With money we can buy goods and services not only for ourselves, but for our future generations: our children, grandchildren, community groups, or institutions we wish to make our beneficiary. In this way, money can change the world.

- **Money has multiple meanings in our society.**

  - **Money can mean power.** In Western culture, *money talks.* You can buy your way into certain privileges and positions of power, control, authority, and influence. You can use money to become a major shareholder in a company and control important business decisions. You can use money to create social change—by building a school or library, by funding cancer research, or even by running for president. Money has power when you use it to make things happen.

  - **Money can mean status, worth, or beauty.** When you tell someone *you look like a million bucks,* you're giving them a double compliment: they look fabulous, and they have great value. In our society, money is equated with worth, status, and beauty. Rich people are admired; poor people are looked down upon. Women with children still earn 30 percent less than men. What does this say about the status or worth of women in our society?

  - **Money can be used as a symbol for love or violence.** Money can be offered and accepted as an expression of love, (you write a generous check as a graduation present for your favorite niece or nephew), or it can be withheld or rejected as an expression of violence (cutting your son or daughter out of your will because they did not conform to your values or life goals). The latter form of violence involves intrusiveness, domination, and control.

  - **Money can be connected to spirituality.** While money is the chief representation of the material world, with roots in our physical needs, bodies, desires, and fears, spirituality represents the *higher* world of transcendence and compassion, the search for meaning, oneness, and community.

The need for balance between the two aspects of our nature has been addressed by spiritual leaders for centuries. Jewish, Christian, Buddhist, American Indian, and many other groups have developed norms for using economic gain not only to satisfy your own needs but to give back to your community, share your wealth or good fortune with others, show compassion, and promote justice. In this way, *having* money is not sinful, but hoarding it just for yourself is considered wrong.

Money can create new desires. Sometimes the more we get, the more we want. Satisfying your wants leaves a void that you want to fill. You've built the house of your dreams, now what? The excitement and newness of it all is wearing off, and you start to dream of a deck or a swimming pool or a trip overseas. These wants can turn into cravings which make you feel out of control, unable to stop or say no to yourself.

3. Distribute the **Attitudes toward Money** checklists and invite participants to reflect on their general attitudes toward money.

   ➤ For questions 1–9, mark the frequency that best describes how often you experience the attitude described.

     ➤ R = Rarely, S = Sometimes, O = Often.

   ➤ For questions 10 and 11, write your responses to the questions in the space provided.

4. Distribute two copies of the **Gender, Money, and Power Issues** questionnaire and guide participants in reflecting on these issues in their family of origin.

   ➤ Use one questionnaire to write your perceptions of the way gender, money, and power were handled in your family of origin—the family in which you grew up.

     ➤ Identify the values held by your family of origin by *underlining* the values your family espoused or lived out by their actions.

     ➤ Identify the specific value of each parent by writing an **M** beside those your mother held and an **F** beside those of your father.

5. When nearly all have finished, ask participants to turn to the second copy of the questionnaire and answer the questions again, this time in relationship to their current family situation.

6. As people are finishing, encourage them to reflect on the similarities and differences between their family of origin issues and their current

marital/family issues. Distribute the **Current Marital/Family Issues** worksheets and give instructions for this final reflection.

➤ Write your responses to the eight questions about your current family situation and issues.

　➤ Move along quickly, trusting your first responses, without trying too hard to analyze or censor your thoughts.

　　☞ *Remind people that there are no right answers. The purpose of the questionnaires is to tease into awareness reflections about attitudes, values, and behaviors. Tell them not to worry if they don't know how to respond to a particular item; perhaps discussion later on will shed light on the issue.*

7. Divide the group into men and women (or several small groups of men and women) and give guidelines for discussion.

　➤ First, all the men sit in a circle and discuss your responses to the questionnaires while the women sit in an outer circle surrounding you and listen. (5 minutes)

　➤ Then reverse the circles so the women are in the center and discuss your responses to the questionnaires while the men sit in the outer circle surrounding you and listen. (5 minutes)

　　☞ *Call time when 5 minutes are up and it's time for men and women to reverse positions in the discussion circles.*

8. Invite responses from men and women's circles as to what they learned about gender similarities and differences in response to issues of gender, money, and power.

9. Divide into mixed gender groups of four to six people to explore possible solutions to problems related to gender, money, and power. (6–8 minutes)

　　☞ *Count off by fours or sixes. If possible, have at least one man and one woman in each group. If either gender is under-represented, ask minority gender individuals to spread out among different groups to help create a gender balance in each group.*

　➤ Find a place to sit down together with your group.

　➤ Take 5 minutes to brainstorm ideas about what constitutes an equal partnership between men and women in terms of money and power.

　➤ The person with the *least* amount of money in their pocket or purse should act as group reporter. Take notes and be ready to report back to the large group on ideas generated by your group.

10. When group discussions seem to be winding down or 5 minutes are up, ask group reporters to share their team's ideas with the large group. List key ideas on newsprint or a blackboard. When each group has given their presentation, invite participants to reflect on possibilities for changing gender, money, and power dynamics in their current family or work situation.

> Look over the list of ideas generated by all groups, and see if you can find an idea you'd like to try in your own family or work situation.

   - Look for possibilities that are most interesting or intriguing to you, and make a mental note of at least one you'd like to try in the next week.

11. Ask if anyone would like to share their plans for change. Then end the session by encouraging people to pay attention to these important issues of gender, money, and power.

● **More marriages or close relationships break up because of money than any other reason.** Couples who have been surveyed report that they fight more about money than anything else, including sex or in-laws. And resentment about the way money is handled is probably the single most important issue separating parents and children, brother and sister. So it's important to be aware of your own issues regarding gender, money, and power—and takes steps necessary to solve the relationship problems that can develop around these issues.

VARIATION

▨ Alternative topics for discussion in *Step 9:*

How an equal partnership in terms of money and power would affect—both positively and negatively—their current relationships.

Ideas for changing one small way in which they participate—either in family relations or with families or origin—in uncomfortable interactions around money and power.

Contributed by Helen Coale, LCSW, LMFT.

ATTITUDES TOWARD MONEY Checklist

	R	S	O
1. I feel like I work to spend.	☐	☐	☐
2. I feel guilty about the way I make money.	☐	☐	☐
3. I feel chronic anxiety about money.	☐	☐	☐
4. I worry about my financial well-being in the future.	☐	☐	☐
5. I resist thinking or talking about money.	☐	☐	☐
6. I define my self-worth, in part, by how much money I make.	☐	☐	☐
7. I feel satisfied with my income or standard of living.	☐	☐	☐
8. I hesitate talking about money with men.	☐	☐	☐
9. I hesitate talking about money with women.	☐	☐	☐

10. In what ways does my gender affects my attitudes toward money?

11. What are my views about the relationship between money and power in relationships?

CURRENT MARITAL/FAMILY ISSUES

What values do I want to teach my children about work? about money?

Is my approach to work and money consistent with what I want to teach my children?

How does gender affect the way my partner and I manage money?

Do my partner and I argue about money as a way of avoiding some other kind of conflict?

Do my partner and I argue about something else in order to avoid discussions of money and power?

How similar/different are my partner's views about money in relation to my own?

How similar/different are my partner's views about power in relation to my own?

GENDER, MONEY, AND POWER ISSUES

A. Does my family talk about money? not talk about money?

B. If my family talks about money, is it only with certain people? in certain contexts? in certain ways? Is this different for men and for women?

C. Do people in my family fight about money either directly or indirectly? Is this different for men and for women?

D. What is the value and meaning of money in my family (self-esteem, money is *dirty*, power/control, success, etc.)? Are values different for men and women?

E. Does my family worry about not having enough? If so, is this reality-based, or would they worry regardless of how much they have? Is this different for men and for women?

F. Do any of the following kinds of money conversations with my family make me anxious: How much I make, how much any other family members makes, how much I spend, how much any other family member spends, how I make my money.

G. Who controls the money in my family? How does this control relate to power distribution in my family of origin?

H. Is money used to cushion against loss? demonstrate equality? handle anger? Is this different for men and for women?

I. If members of my family knew everything about the way I earn, spend, and manage money, what would they be pleased with? upset or disapproving about? Is this different for men and for women in my family?

J. Are there obligations connected with money/success? Are these different for men and for women?

K. Does my sibling position affect my family's expectations of me regarding money or success?

L. Which of the following values are held by my family?
- ☐ public service vs. self-interest
- ☐ promptness vs. procrastination re: bill paying
- ☐ hard work vs. indulgence/entitlement
- ☐ busyness vs. leisure
- ☐ consumerism vs. thrift
- ☐ entrepreneurial vs. salaried employment
- ☐ risk-taking (financial/other) vs. safety
- ☐ work/money as a way of defining successful self vs. character, behavior as definition of success
- ☐ self-made vs. indulged

23 WORKING PARTNERS: DREAM SHARING

This simple process for couples gets to the heart of all successful part-
nerships: shared vision, commitment, and conflict resolution.

GOALS

To clarify individual values and goals, prioritize them, and share dreams
with partners.

To develop a shared vision with partners and work as a team to achieve
common goals.

GROUP SIZE

Unlimited. For couples only.

TIME FRAME

50–60 minutes.

MATERIALS NEEDED

Goals and Dreams worksheet; **Partnership Plan** worksheet; (optional:
trainer's handout on conflict resolution steps or skills).

PROCESS

☞ *This process assumes that couples have had previous training, education, or information about conflict resolution. It might be helpful to
review the basic steps of conflict resolutions and provide a handout.*

1. Begin the session with an icebreaker to help people get acquainted.
   (6–8 minutes)

   ➤ Turn to your partner and each of you recall a time in the past when
   you worked successfully as a team to accomplish a common goal.
   Take a minute to share these memories.

   ☞ *Interrupt after 1 minute.*

   ➤ Now join with another couple you don't know well and introduce
   yourselves by telling each other your success stories.

   – Describe what you did that worked well and the role that each
   of you played in helping achieve your goal.

   – Take 5 minutes in all to tell your stories.

2. Invite folks to share examples of goals achieved through teamwork

with partners. Then summarize the value of teamwork in a short chalktalk.

- **Partners who work on common goals are more likely to be successful.** By developing a shared vision of what is most important to you and creating a plan for achieving these goals, you are more likely to say *yes* to important things and *no* to things unrelated to your goal. This keeps you on track and is a wise use of your resources.

- **Before you develop shared goals, it is important to know your individual goals.** You need to know what *you* want before you can negotiate a common goal with your partner. You need to know your personal and occupational goals as well as your dreams and values or what's really important to you.

3. Distribute the **Goals and Dreams** worksheets to each participant and provide guidelines for personal reflection about what each person wants in terms of material objects, skills or learning, and life experiences/quality of life over the next three years. (5–6 minutes)

   ➤ Write today's date in the space at the top.

   ➤ For your goal date, write the date it will be three years from today.

   ➤ In the goal boxes labelled **A, B,** and **C,** make a list of your goals— everything you want to **own or possess**, skills you want to **learn**, or **experiences** you want to try by your goal date.

      ➤ Do not censor any of your wants or worry about if they are realistic at this time. List as many as you can, as honestly as possible, without judging yourself.

      ➤ In list **A,** write down all the material objects you want to own or possess three years from now (financial savings, living room furniture, new car, etc.).

      ➤ In list **B,** write down all the skills or learning you want to have achieved three years from now (computer skills, country dancing, better communications, etc.).

      ➤ In list **C,** write down experiences or quality of life you hope to enjoy by your goal date (time with children, improved health, solitude, trip to Australia, etc.).

4. When most people have full lists, invite folks to reflect on the relative importance of their various goals.

   ➤ Look over your three lists of goals and mark with a * those that are most important to you.

☞ *Wait until people have marked goals before going on.*

➤ Look over your marked goals. Select your *ten most important goals* and transfer them to list **D**, ranking them in order of their impor- tance to you, putting the most important at the top of the list and the tenth most important at the bottom.

5. Invite couples to share their discoveries with each other. (4–5 minutes)

➤ Pair up with your partner and take turns sharing your personal goals and dreams from lists **A, B,** and **C.**

➢ Do not judge, criticize, or debate your partner's goals or dreams. Simply listen and learn what is important to your partner.

➤ Before disclosing your top ten list, try to guess each other's top three goals. How accurate were you in guessing your partner's needs?

6. Ask volunteers to share examples of goals or dreams they shared in common with their partners. Use this as a lead in to the next part of the exercise—creating a shared vision and developing a plan for achiev- ing common goals. Hand out the **Partnership Plan** worksheets and give instructions. (8–10 minutes)

☞ *Walk couples through each step of the process. Invite questions and offer assistance if people get stuck. If necessary, give a short role-play demonstration of conflict-resolution skills and/ or share conflict resolution handouts, if available.*

➤ As a couple, review your individual top ten goals again, looking for goals you have in common.

➤ Out of the twenty total goals generated by the two of you, decide on three goals from your lists that you want to work on together.

➢ The goals can be from any category or combination of categories you want (material goals, learning goals, experiential goals).

➢ The important thing is that the goals you pick are ones that are important to both of you and are goals you are both willing to commit time and money resources toward achieving.

➤ Write the three goals in the appropriate space of your **Partnership Plan** worksheet. Material goals go under statement **A**, learning/ skill goals go under statement **B**, and life experience goals go under statement **C**.

➢ You may have more than three goals, but for now focus on only *three shared goals.*

~ You may have one goal of each type, all three goals in the same area, or some other mixture.

> *Pause until everyone has agreed on goals and written them down on their worksheet.*

> After you have agreed on three common goals and have written them on your worksheet, briefly discuss the amount of resources—time and money—that you will need to achieve these goals.

~ Write your estimates about resources needed to achieve each goal in the spaces provided in section **D** for **Estimated Resources**, then add the totals for resources needed.

> *Allow 2–3 minutes.*

> Now comes the hard part—action. Imagine yourselves as small business owners. The success of your business strongly depends on both partners and your ability or willingness to commit time, energy, and money to the future growth of the business. Teamwork is essential for success and satisfaction with outcome.

~ What will each of you do to help your partnership achieve your goals?

> *Ask for volunteers to share examples of goals and invite the group to brainstorm ideas for achieving those goals (a second job, redistribution of family chores, following a budget, bartering for childcare, etc.). Then encourage couples to make their own commitments.*

> In section **E,** write at least six steps you will take either individually (with partner's support) or jointly to help achieve your goals.

~ Work toward a balance of activity, effort, or commitment by each partner so you can have a sense of teamwork and shared responsibility for achieving goals.

~ When you have agreed on six steps or actions, you may want to strengthen your working partnership by each person signing the plan.

7. Reconvene the group and solicit observations and insights, using a few open-ended questions.

✓ What were some surprise discoveries you made today?

✓ What was most striking to you about your personal goals and dreams or those you and your partner had in common?

✓ What did you learn from this experience?

✓ How do you think you will use this learning?

> *Some couples will discover they have more wants and needs than time or money. Reassure people that wanting more than we have is a normal, perhaps even universal, human response. This is why clarifying goals and values is so important.*

8. Close with a summary of principles for mutual goal-setting and a peptalk encouraging participants to practice dream-sharing on a regular basis.

VARIATIONS

▓ If you have time during the icebreaker, ask couples to discuss personal goals or motivations for attending this workshop. Solicit a few examples and relate them to your agenda. Then point out the value of knowing personal goals and values before developing shared goals.

▓ Incorporate an expanded section on conflict-resolution skills into the session after *Step 5*. Use a brief chalktalk on key principles, skills, or steps followed by a role-play demonstration and practice in quads (pair up two couples).

GOALS AND DREAMS

Today's date: _____   Goal date: _____

A. Material objects
*financial savings, furniture, new
car, etc.*

_____

_____

_____

_____

_____

_____

_____

_____

_____

C. Experiences/quality of life
*time with children, solitude, trip
to Australia, etc.*

_____

_____

_____

_____

_____

_____

_____

_____

B. Skills
*word processing, country dancing,
communication skills, etc.*

_____

_____

_____

_____

_____

_____

_____

_____

★ ★ **Top ten goals** ★ ★

1. _____
       most important

2. _____

3. _____

4. _____

5. _____

6. _____

7. _____

8. _____

9. _____

10. _____
        least important

PARTNERSHIP PLAN

A. By (year) _____, we will own/possess the following **material objects:**

B. and/or will have **learned** the following **skills:**

C. and/or will have enjoyed the following **life experiences** or quality of life:

D. Estimated resources for achieving the above goals are

       Goal 1: (time)_____   (money) _____

       Goal 2: (time)_____   (money) _____

       Goal 3: (time)_____   (money) _____

  Total needed: (time)_____   (money) _____

E. In order to achieve these goals, we agreed to work as partners to do the following:

    1. _____

    2. _____

    3. _____

    4. _____

    5. _____

    6. _____

Signed: _____ and _____

24 YOUR BOSS IS NOT YOUR MOTHER

In this innovative exercise, participants identify work relationships most likely to trigger reenactments of family of origin patterns and explore possibilities for changing these patterns.

GOALS

To explore how family of origin roles and family system dynamics impact workplace behavior and job satisfaction.

To identify work situations that trigger the use of childhood coping strategies and plan for changing problem relationships.

GROUP SIZE

Unlimited.

TIME FRAME

60–75 minutes.

MATERIALS NEEDED

Family Roles worksheets; newsprint and marker.

PROCESS

☞ *This exercise is most appropriate for groups of people who do not know each other or work together. Do not use it with groups of coworkers unless issues of confidentiality have been addressed and you are sure that the work environment is a safe place for people to explore these sensitive issues.*

1. Begin with a series of provocative questions to help people tune in to possible symptoms of family dynamics spilling over into the workplace.

   ✔ Do your relationships at work often leave you feeling beaten up, discouraged, or vaguely angry at the end of the day?

   ✔ Do you ever find yourself speaking and acting in ways that feel inappropriate or out of proportion to the situation (e.g., blowing your stack, yelling at your boss, crying in the supply closet)?

   ✔ Do you get stuck sometimes in no-win situations that keep you from doing your job well and make you look bad?

✓ Do you regularly feel bullied, disrespected, manipulated, or pushed around by certain people?

● **You are not alone.** Most people experience uncomfortable moments like this at work on an occasional basis, or even frequently. Whenever we experience these symptoms, it is likely that we are responding to work stress by using emotional and behavioral patterns we learned as a child for responding to stress in our family.

● And while we may have also developed a whole range of healthier patterns over the years, at times of stress at work, those hidden, unhealthy behaviors of the past get triggered once again. After all, they are the ones we used as children **to cover up stressful feelings and maintain control.**

2. Invite people to consider their own work situations as you describe seven signals that old family patterns are surfacing at work.

● **Not all family patterns are bad!** A lot of the skills and patterns that you learned as a child probably continue to serve you very well as an adult. Growing up in a family teaches us how to become adults. Most of your best talents have their roots in your family of origin. You may even have selected your profession based on your family roles. Celebrate your marvelous inheritance.

● **But family patterns can also cause us trouble.** This exercise focuses on those childhood patterns that don't work so well as an adult and are especially troublesome when you use them at work. Most of us have at least a few of those habits as well. They are the behaviors that tend to get us into difficulty as adults. Consider the seven typical patterns at work.

● **Repetition.** If you find yourself fighting the same battles over and over again (usually unsuccessfully) or consistently reacting in the same way to certain situations or people, it's likely that you are engaging in an emotional dynamic you learned long ago in your family. This is especially likely if others around you respond differently to the same triggers.

● **Blaming or obsessing.** If your find yourself focusing on the faults of coworkers or obsessing about incidents or interactions, it's likely you're on the defensive because of an old family pattern. Does this person remind you of someone in your family? Do your feelings in the situation echo childhood emotions?

● **Feeling anxious, afraid, angry, or confused.** Watch out for these telltale emotions at work. They're almost certain to stem from defensive reactions you learned at an early age—ones that are now counterproductive as an adult in the workplace.

● **Taking on conflicts or problems of others.** If you find yourself trying to patch up conflicts around the office, beware! When you take on others' problems, you usually end up responding in inappropriate ways that get you in trouble at work.

● **Feeling restricted.** If you're feeling limited by an individual or situation on the job, consider the parallels with your past family experience. It's likely that your present reaction is likely out of proportion for the current reality.

● **Provoking others.** If you frequently experience manipulative, controlling, defensive reactions from others, it's likely that your old family survival patterns are having a ripple effect on the people around you.

● **Resisting change.** Watch your reactions under stress, when policies, working conditions, procedures, routines, or schedules change. Are you responding with an old habit of defending yourself that's leftover from your childhood family role?

3. Invite participants to recall uncomfortable or upsetting situations from their work setting where old family patterns may be showing up.

 ➤ Think back over the past week or so at work and identify one or more situations when you experienced "icky" feelings that took you by surprise—anxiety, frustration, uncertainty, irritation, impotence, outrage, hurt, confusion, feeling left out or put down or put upon.

 ➤ Pair up with a neighbor and take turns describing one of those situations. You will have 2 minutes for this process.

4. Solicit examples from the group and use them to introduce and illustrate the concepts of family and work systems. Elaborate on how stress at work often provokes people into replaying family dynamics.

● **Workplace systems often resemble family systems.** Whenever people come together in groups they tend to re-create the emotional dynamics of family. This is especially true at work where we see each other almost every day, spend long periods of time together, and to some extent are emotionally and economically dependent on each other. Even if we don't like each other, we have to get along and work together to reach a common goal.

● **Workplaces, like families, have built-in power differentials.** Like a teenager in a family who is both independent and dependent, you probably have some degree of autonomy in your work but also various authority figures or subsystems to which you are accountable. Unless you are the boss, someone else is in charge, setting the rules for you to follow, and you have to live with the consequences.

- **Like a family, a work system is usually composed of several subsystems.** With the similarity in structure and dynamics, it's no wonder we find ourselves reenacting familiar family roles and getting hooked emotionally at work.

- **Under stress on the job, we instinctively revert to roles and behaviors we learned in our families.** We pout. We squabble. We clam up. We compete for attention. We gang up on each other. We disrupt and sabotage. We poke and prod. We form alliances and subsystems. We act helpless. We revel. We lash out. We dig in our heels. We whine. We blame. We deny our responsibility. We try to please. We give the cold shoulder. We bully. We are sneaky. We butt in where we don't belong. We pretend everything is just fine.

- **Family roles backfire at work.** Although these responses might have been effective (at least occasionally) to defend ourselves at home, they are usually nonproductive in the workplace. Instead of helping us feel secure, loved, valued, and important, these defense mechanisms can be downright dangerous at work. Indulging in old roles narrows our options for responding to work challenges. Emotional baggage interferes with our effectiveness and productivity. When we indulge in childlike behaviors, we generate toxic feelings such as anger, frustration, powerlessness, and anxiety, contaminating the environment for everyone.

5. Distribute the **Family Roles** worksheets. Review the concept of family roles, elaborating on the sixteen common roles listed at the top.

- Whatever system we're in, we usually take on a typical role that is grounded in how we learned to operate best in our family system. These roles are really a pattern of relating and interacting that we originally developed unconsciously as emotional survival tools, devised to help us feel loved, cherished, important, and secure. As adults, we often fall back on these habitual roles to help us cope in stressful situations.

6. Invite participants to reflect on the roles they typically played in their family of origin.

- ➤ Look over the list of roles and mark with an **F** the roles you remember yourself frequently taking **in your family of origin**.

➤ Mark your three or four most typical roles.

7. Invite participants to reflect on the roles they find themselves playing at work.

   ● Research documents the powerful **link between family roles we learn in childhood and our reactions and behaviors as adults.** Our habit of responding to family stress in certain ways predisposes us to acting out these same roles again as adults when the emotional climate and demands of the situation seem similar.

   ➤ Look over the list at the top of your worksheet again and mark roles you recognize yourself taking **at work**. Mark them with a **W.**

   ➤ Now look at the list of roles again and decide which roles bother or upset you most when others at work use them with you.

      ➤ Which three are most likely to provoke your own childish reaction? And who plays these roles?

   ➤ What overlap do you see between your ways of relating at work and how you related in your family of origin?

8. Invite people to explore specific examples of how family roles have spilled into their workplace and the resulting consequences.

   ➤ Transfer three of the roles you marked with a **W** to the left column at the bottom of your worksheet.

      ➤ Pick the three roles you most often play at work.

   ➤ In the middle column, describe a specific instance of that role in action, a situation when you acted out this role at work recently.

   ➤ In the right column note some of the consequences of your taking that role. Looking back at the situation, what impact did your behavior have on others? On you? On your work and your workplace?

9. Ask people to find a partner with no more than one work role they share in common. Instruct pairs to spend 5 minutes discussing examples of how they sometimes enact their old family roles at work.

10. Reconvene the group and help people make resolutions for change.

   ● **Family roles and childlike behavior in the workplace signal the need for change.** They flash the warning that old family patterns are surfacing at work and you need to shift into adult mode to create a more satisfying and productive work climate.

   ➤ If you had a magic wand, what roles and dynamics would you like to change at work? Turn your worksheet over and make your wish list for change.

> Identify two or three stressful work relationships that you're worried or concerned about (a situation that makes you feel uncomfortable, times when you find yourself reverting to childish roles, a person you feel disconnected from, a relationship you feel disappointed with because it isn't more positive, etc.).

11. Invite participants to consider possible consequences of change before committing themselves to action.

● **Take responsibility.** You are the only one who can change. You can't change another person's attitudes, feelings, or behavior. If you want things to be different, you need to start by looking inside yourself rather than by blaming others.

● **Consider the consequences.** Anytime you initiate change, you are taking a risk. In emotional tangles at work, it's dangerous to attempt changes when the stress level of the situation is high—or with people who have significant emotional influence (positive or negative) over you. Evaluate the possible outcomes before you attempt any change.

● **Make smart decisions.** Since family dynamics and roles are so powerful and persistent in our lives, and systems are so resistant to change, it makes sense to start with low risk changes. Avoid high risk changes, if possible.

● **Make small changes.** Save major changes for low risk relationships where you are less vulnerable. Make minor adjustments that can have a major positive impact. Eat in the lunchroom instead of at your desk. Practice cheerfulness. Sit next to someone you usually avoid. Try countering complaints with appreciation. Count to ten before blowing up. Say no occasionally.

12. Ask people to choose one work relationship they want to improve.

> Write the person's initials on your worksheet.

> Now consider possibilities for changing your attitude, feelings, or behavior in your relationship with this person.

 ⟩ Write three ideas for changing your relationship and interactions with this person: one for changing your **attitude**, one for changing your **feelings**, and one for changing your **behavior**.

 ⟩ Put a star by the idea you like best and would consider trying in the next month.

13. Ask people to solidify their commitment to change by sharing their plans for change with another person.

© 1997 Whole Person Associates 210 W Michigan Duluth, MN 55802 (800) 247-6789

14. After 2–3 minutes, interrupt the conversations and ask for examples of plans for change. Then give a closing peptalk on tips for making successful changes in work relationships.

● **Learn how to relax.** Practice deep breathing, soothing self-talk, or other methods of calming yourself down in a crisis so that you can think more clearly.

● **Learn to communicate respectfully.** Practice expressing yourself in ways that convey respect for the other person: listening closely, not interrupting, avoiding judging, accusing, or blaming tactics, etc. Your overall attitude, tone of voice, and body posture will be less threatening when you approach others respectfully.

● **Consider timing.** Think carefully about the appropriate time and place to initiate changes or bring up difficult topics. A staff meeting is not the time or place to bring up a personal conflict with your supervisor. Your chances for success will be greater when you schedule a time that is private and convenient for both of you.

● **Avoid power plays.** They are likely to trigger other people's defensive patterns. Avoid language and behavior that could be construed as intimidating or manipulative. Use "I" language and take responsibility for yourself, your feelings, and your behavior. Don't blame others for your problems.

● **Break your old family rules.** Try new roles. If your role was that of the *martyr*, and the rule was *"suffer in silence,"* remind yourself that you have the right to speak up and ask for what you want. Suffering in silence only hurts you and interferes with your ability to do your job effectively.

● **Remember to assess the risks of change,** especially in work relationships with people who have strong positive or negative emotional influence with you. A lot is at stake in these relationships—perhaps even your job.

● **Focus on yourself.** If you try to change others, you're setting yourself up for frustration and stress. You can't control others or change their behavior. Remember, they learned some odd patterns of reacting in their families, too! You can control yourself and your own behavior. This is where you should direct your energy. When you do, you'll probably feel better about yourself and your work.

Concepts in this exercise are adapted from Brian DesRoches's invaluable book, Your Boss Is Not Your Mother *(New York: Avon Books, 1995).*

FAMILY ROLES

SUPERACHIEVER
Brings glory to everyone by doing well. Whizkid. Perfectionist.

HERO
Always in the limelight. Looks wonderful. Beyond reproach.

"GOOD" KID
Quiet. Perfect. "Brown noser." Doesn't rock the boat. Nearly invisible.

PEOPLE PLEASER
Bends over backward to keep everyone happy. Anticipates other's needs.

CHEERLEADER
Always positive and upbeat. Refuses to acknowledge conflict or problems.

VICTIM
Acts helpless. Easily hurt by others. Whines and blames.

RESCUER
Always on the lookout for someone to save. Do-gooder.

PERSECUTER
Exerts power over others, often inflicting pain. Dumps the problem on others.

REBEL
Challenges authority and the status quo. Always plays devil's advocate.

SCAPEGOAT
Assumes blame for the problem.

"BAD" KID
Breaks the rules. Acts out negatively. Troublemaker.

MASCOT
Everyone's darling or pet. A charm who doesn't have to be responsible.

CLOWN
Uses humor to dispel tension or distract others from conflict or problems.

MARTYR
Absorbs pain like a sponge. Takes on the problems of the system. Suffers with or without complaining.

CAREGIVER
Focuses on solving others' problems while ignoring own. Mother hen.

TYRANT
Uses power to coerce others to do what the tyrant wants regardless of the effects.

Role	Work example	Consequences

© 1997 Whole Person Associates 210 W Michigan Duluth, MN 55802   (800) 247-6789

resources

RESOURCE BIBLIOGRAPHY

Anderson, Carol M., and Susan Stewart. *Flying Solo: Single Women in Midlife*. New York: W.W. Norton & Company, 1994.

Bank, Stephen P., and Michael D. Kahn. *The Sibling Bond*. New York: Basic Books, 1982.

Biffle, Christopher. *A Journey through Your Childhood*. Los Angeles: Jeremy P. Tarcher, 1989.

Bozarth-Campbell, Alla. *Life is Goodbye, Life is Hello*. Minneapolis, Minn.: CompCare Publishers, 1982.

Buscaglia, Leo F. *Living, Loving, & Learning*. New York: Fawcett Columbine, 1982.

Carter, Elizabeth A., and Monica McGoldrick, eds. *The Family Life Cycle: A Framework for Family Therapy*. New York: Gardner Press, 1980.

Carter, Jaine and James D. Carter. *He Works She Works: Successful Strategies for Working Couples*. New York: American Management Association, 1995.

Clark, Don. *Loving Someone Gay*. Berkeley, Calif.: Celestial Arts, 1987.

Clarke, Jean Illsley. *Self-Esteem: A Family Affair*. Minneapolis, Minn.: Winston Press, 1978.

Clinebell, Howard, and Doris Clinebell. *The Intimate Marriage*. New York: Harper & Row, 1970.

Covington, Stephanie. *Awakening Your Sexuality: A Guide for Recovering Women and Their Partners*. San Francisco: HarperSanFrancisco, 1991.

Covington, Stephanie, and Liana Beckett. *Leaving the Enchanted Forest*. San Francisco: Harper & Row, 1988.

Curran, Dolores. *Stress and the Healthy Family*. New York: HarperPaperbacks, 1985.

——. *Traits of a Healthy Family*. Minneapolis, Minn.: Winston Press, 1983.

DesRoches, Brian. *Your Boss Is Not Your Mother*. New York: Avon Books, 1995.

Doub, George T., and Virginia Morgan Scott. *Family Wellness Workbook*. Santa Cruz, Calif.: Family Wellness Associates, 1987.

Dunne, Pam Barragar. *The Narrative Therapist and the Arts*. Los Angeles: Possibilities Press, 1992.

Elliott, Barbara A., Kathryn C. Halvorson, and Marybeth K. Hendricks-Matthews. *Family Violence and Abusive Relationships,* Primary Care: Clinics in Office Practice series, Philadelphia, Pa.: W.B. Saunders Company, 1993.

Elliott, Barbara, and Sharon Price. *Vision 2010: Families and Health Care*. Minneapolis, Minn.: National Council on Family Relations, 1993.

Fairchild, Betty, and Nancy Hayward. *Now That You Know: What Every Parent Should Know about Homosexuality*. New York: Harcourt Brace Jovanovich, 1989.

Fossum, Merle A., and Marilyn J. Mason. *Facing Shame: Families in Recovery*. New York: W.W. Norton & Company, 1986.

Foster, Carolyn. *The Family Patterns Workbook*. Los Angeles: Jeremy P. Tarcher, 1993.

Hendrix, Harville. *Getting the Love You Want: A Guide for Couples*. New York, HarperPerennial, 1988.

Hetherington, Cheryl. *Working with Groups from Dysfunctional Families*. Duluth, Minn.: Whole Person Associates, 1994.

Imber-Black, Evan, and Janine Roberts. *Rituals for Our Times*. New York: HarperPerennial, 1992.

Jewett, Claudia L. *Helping Children Cope with Separation and Loss.* Cambridge, Mass.: Harvard Common Press, 1982.

Krause, Carol. *How Healthy Is Your Family Tree?* New York: Fireside, 1995.

LeFevre, Dale N. *New Games for the Whole Family.* New York: Perigee Books, 1988.

Louden, Jennifer. *The Couple's Comfort Book.* San Francisco: HarperSanFrancisco, 1994.

Lysne, Robin Heerens. *Dancing Up the Moon: A Woman's Guide to Creating Traditions that Bring Sacredness to Daily Life.* Berkeley, Calif.: Conari Press, 1995.

Madanes, Cloé, and Claudio Madanes. *The Secret Meaning of Money.* San Francisco: Jossey-Bass Publishers, 1994.

Marston, Stephanie. *The Divorced Parent.* New York: Pocket Books, 1994.

Mason, Marilyn J. *Making Our Lives Our Own.* New York: HarperCollins, 1991.

McConnell, Patty. *A Workbook for Healing: Adult Children of Alcoholics.* San Francisco: Harper & Row, 1986.

McGoldrick, Monica, and Randy Gerson. *Genograms in Family Assessment.* New York: W.W. Norton & Company, 1985.

McKay, Matthew, et al. *The Divorce Book.* Oakland, Calif.: New Harbinger, 1984.

McKay, Matthew, Martha Davis, and Patrick Fanning. *Messages: The Communication Book.* Oakland, Calif.: New Harbinger, 1983.

McNaught, Brian. *On Being Gay.* New York: St. Martin's Press, 1988.

Moore, Thomas. *Soul Mates.* New York: HarperPerennial, 1994.

Napier, Augustus Y. *The Fragile Bond.* New York: Harper & Row, 1988.

Papernow, Patricia L. *Becoming a Stepfamily: Patterns of Development in Remarried Families.* San Francisco, Calif.: Jossey-Bass, 1993.

Pence, Ellen, and Michael Paymar. *Education Groups for Men Who Batter: The Duluth Model.* New York: Springer Publishing, 1993.

Reddy, Maureen T., Martha Roth, and Amy Sheldon, eds. *Mother Journeys: Feminists Write about Mothering.* Minneapolis, Minn.: Spinsters Ink, 1994.

Roberts, Janine. *Tales and Transformations: Stories in Families and Family Therapy.* New York: W.W. Norton & Company, 1994.

Satir, Virginia. *Conjoint Family Therapy.* Palo Alto, Calif.: Science and Behavior Books, 1967.

————*The New Peoplemaking.* Mountain View, Calif.: Science and Behavior Books, 1988.

Tannen, Deborah. *You Just Don't Understand: Women and Men in Conversation.* New York: Ballantine Books, 1990.

Toman, Walter, PhD. *Family Constellation.* New York: Springer Publishing, 1976.

Tubesing, Donald A. and Nancy Loving Tubesing. *Seeking Your Healthy Balance.* Duluth, Minn.: Whole Person Associates, 1991.

Walters, Marianne, Betty Carter, Peggy Papp, and Olga Silverstein. *The Invisible Web.* New York: Guilford Press, 1988.

Whitfield, Charles L, MD. *Boundaries and Relationships: Knowing, Protecting, and Enjoying the Self.* Deerfield Beach, Fla.: Health Communications, 1993.

Wolin, Steven J., and Sybil Wolin. *The Resilient Self.* New York: Villard Books, 1993.

CONTRIBUTORS

Sandy Stewart Christian, MSW, LICSW. 3215 Queen, Missoula MT 59801. 406-549-3602. Editor *of Structured Exercises in Wellness Promotion Volume 5, Structured Exercises in Stress Management Volume 5, Working with Groups to Explore Food and Body Connections,* and *Instant Icebreakers.* Sandy is a licensed marriage and family therapist. She is a clinical member of the American Association of Marriage and Family Therapy and has conducted numerous workshops and training events for human service professionals and community groups.

Helen W. Coale, LCSW, LMFT. Atlanta Area Child Guidance Clinic, 17-B Lenox Pointe NE, Atlanta GA 30324. 404-261-2265. Helen has practiced clinical social work and marriage and family therapy in Atlanta since 1969. She is the author of numerous articles on family therapy, child welfare, stepfamilies, humor in therapy, and brief therapy, and is the author of *All About Families the Second Time Around* (Peachtree Publishers, 1980). She is an adjunct faculty member of the University of Georgia School of Social Work and a local and national presenter on family therapy, brief therapy, stepfamilies, the significance of money in families and in client/therapist relationships, and professional ethics.

Stephanie S. Covington, PhD, LCSW. 7946 Ivanhoe Ave, Suite 201B, la Jolla CA 92037. 858-454-8528. Stephanie is a psychotherapist. author, and consultant recognized for her pioneering work on women's issues. She specializes in trainings on addiction, sexuality, and relationships. Educated at Columbia University and the Union Institute, she has taught at the graduate level and conducted seminars internationally. Her consulting work includes the design of the women's treatment program at the Betty Ford Center. Stephanie has authored *Leaving the Enchanted Forest: The Path from Relationship Addiction to Intimacy; Awakening Your Sexuality: A Guide for Recovering Women and Their Partners;* and *A Woman's Way through the Twelve Steps.*

Brian DesRoches, PhD. 2800 E Madison St, Suite 302, Seattle WA 98112. 206-323-6114. Brian is a psychotherapist, organization systems consultant, and professional speaker. He is the author of *Your Boss Is Not Your Mother* and *Reclaiming Yourself.* He has graduate degrees in counseling, hospital administration, and business administration, is a clinical member of the American Association of Marriage and Family Therapy, and has extensive experience as a corporate executive in large health care systems. The focus of his work is supporting individuals in experiencing fulfillment and satisfaction through self-awareness, choice, and accountability.

Frederick A. DiBlasio, PhD, LCSW-C. Professor and Therapist. School of Social Work, University of Maryland-Baltimore, 525 W Redwood St, Baltimore MD 21201. 410-706-7799. Frederick did his clinical training session with internationally renowned therapist Harry Aponte and was the chair of the National Conference on Forgiveness in Clinical Practice and a clinical member of the American Association of Marriage and Family Therapy. He has written a book with John Belcher entitled *Helping the Homeless: Where Do We Go from Here?* (New York: Free Press, 1990), has authored over thirty-five professional journal articles and publications, and holds over twenty years of clinical practice experience.

Barbara A. Elliott, PhD. Department of Family Medicine, School of Medicine, University of Minnesota-Duluth, Duluth MN 55812. 218-726-6981. Barbara is known nationally and internationally for her work as a teacher, researcher, writer, and presenter on topics related to families, health, and medicine. She has been honored by Governor Arne Carlson as Minnesota's Marvelous Woman of the Year, by the Duluth Family Practice Residency Program as Teacher of the Year, and has been selected as a Kellog National Leadership Fellow. She is coeditor of *Primary Care: Clinics in Office Practice* (W.B. Saunders Company, 1993) and editor of *Vision 2010: Families and Health Care* (National Council on Family Relations, 1993).

Madge Holmes, RN, PhD. 460 Alma St, Suite 200, Monterey CA 93940. 831-372-7400. Madge is the Graduate Psychology Coordinator at Chapman University in Monterey and has a private marriage and family therapy practice. She has developed many creative workshops combining art and family systems techniques for use in areas of stress and anxiety reduction, resolving traumatic memories, wellness, and relationship enhancement. She is a clinical member of the American Association for Marriage and Family Therapy and the California Association of Marriage and Family Therapists.

Sue Johnson-Douglas, C. Psych. Professor of Psychology and Psychiatry, University of Ottawa, 11 Marie Curie St, PO Box 450, Suite A, Ottawa ON K1N 6N5 Canada. 613-562-5800 x4813. Sue is one of the originators of Emotionally Focused Therapy for couples (Guilford, 1988), which is now the second most empirically validated form of couples treatment in North America. She is also primary editor of *The Heart of the Matter: Emotion in Marital Therapy* (Brunner/Mazel, 1994). Sue conducts research on couples therapy and close relationships. She is also the Director of the Marital and Family Therapy Clinic at the Civic Hospital in Ottawa where she actively trains clinicians from many disciplines in marital and family therapy.

Andrew J. King, MS. Andy develops and conducts training for the volunteers and staff at a gay and lesbian health organization and an AIDS service provider. In addition to recruiting and managing volunteers, he has developed a variety of training programs on HIV and AIDS, safer sex, diversity issues, homophobia, gay and lesbian sensitivity, boundary issues, and volunteer management.

William Madsen, PhD. 51 Kondazian St, Watertown MA 02172. 617-924-2617. Bill is on the faculty of the Family Institute of Cambridge. He has a private therapy practice and provides family therapy training and consultation to agencies and organizations throughout New England. He has written a number of articles on family-centered services and on treatment difficulties that develop between families and providers.

Michael E. Metz, PhD. Meta Resources Institute, Baker Court, Suite 440, 821 Raymond Ave, St. Paul MN 55114. 651-642-9317. Michael is a licensed psychologist and marriage and family therapist, an adjunct assistant professor in the Marriage and Family Program in the Family Social Science department of the University of Minnesota. He is the author of more than twenty-five professional articles on marital and sex therapy, sexual medicine, relationship playfulness, and conflict resolution dynamics. He is also the author of the Styles of Conflict Inventory (SO), a clinical assessment measure of couples' conflict patterns.

Patricia L. Papernow, EdD. 279 Cabot St, Newtonville MA 02160. 617-354-4829. Patricia is a psychologist in private practice in Newton, Massachusetts. She is nationally known for her work on stepfamily development and has frequently appeared on TV and radio and in magazines, journals, and newspapers including *The New York Times, Washington Post,* and *Los Angeles Times.* She conducts numerous workshops across the country on these issues, and is the author of *Becoming a Stepfamily: Patterns of Development in Remarried Families* (San Francisco: Jossey-Bass Publishers, 1993).

Ellen Pence, PhD, ABD. Domestic Abuse Intervention Project, 206 W 4th St, Duluth MN 55806. 218-722-2781. 218-722-0779 (fax). One of the founding mothers of the Domestic Abuse Intervention Project, which has become a national model for coordinated community-based intervention in domestic assault cases, Ellen is an internationally known speaker and writer on domestic violence. She has published numerous articles in national journals and books and is coauthor of *Education Groups for Men Who Batter: The Duluth Model* (New York: Springer, 1993). Ellen is completing her dissertation at the Ontario Institute for the Study of Education at the University of Toronto.

Janine Roberts, EdD. University of Massachusetts-Amherst, Room 159 Hills South, Box 34150, Amherst MA 01003-4150. 413-545-3569. Janine is a professor of family therapy at the University of Massachusetts in Amherst and a board member of the American Family Therapy Academy. She is the author of *Tales and Transformations: Stories in Families and Family Therapy (Norton,* 1994), coeditor of *Rituals in Families and Family Therapy,* and coauthor (with Evan Imber-Black) of *Rituals for Our Times: Celebrating, Healing, and Changing Our Lives and Our Relationships.* She is on the editorial boards of *Family Process, the Journal of Marital and Family Therapy,* and the *Journal of Systemic Therapies* and most recently was the editor of the *Journal of Feminist Family Therapy.*

Virginia Morgan Scott, MSW. 116 Allegro Dr, Santa Cruz CA 95060. 831-426-6734. Virginia has taught in the family education programs at the University of Pittsburgh, California State University, and the University of San Francisco and is cofounder of Family Wellness Associates. She holds thirty years experience as a family therapist and has published *Family Wellness Workbook* (1988) and a video series entitled *Survival Skills for Healthy Families.* For more information on the book or video series, please call 408-427-0722.

Gabriel Smilkstein, MD. Professor, University of California-Davis Department of Family Practice. Before his untimely death, while this volume was in process, Gabe had a long-standing interest in the family and the biopsychological model of health. He was the author of ten textbook chapters in family medicine and over fifty papers in peer reviewed journals. Throughout his professional career, Gabe was a tireless defender of and advocate for family well-being.

Katherine H. Speare, PhD. Center for Psychological Health, 1507 Tower Ave, Suite 210B, Superior WI 54880. 715-394-2920. Katherine is a licensed psychologist with over twenty years experience. In her private practice, Dr. Speare specializes in working with adult women on depression and related issues. For over five years, she has been presenting workshops on boundaries to medical professionals, psychologists, psychotherapists, social service workers, clergy, law enforcement, and chemical dependency professionals. She has provided consultation to various staff groups who are experiencing boundary-related problems. She recently developed and has been presenting a workshop on Women at Mid-life and is currently pursuing research on creativity.

Sally Strosahl, MA. Marriage and Family Therapist, 116 S Westlawn, Aurora IL 60506. 630-897-9796. Sally received an MA in clinical psychology, trained at the Wholistic Health Center, and researched the relationship between stress and illness. In addition to her private practice in marriage and family therapy, Sally frequently presents workshops in the areas of wellness and stress management, burnout prevention, body image and size acceptance, and marriage enrichment. She particularly enjoys working with systems (family, work groups, agencies, businesses, churches) to help enhance each member's growth and well-being. She is the cofounder of ABUNDIA, a service providing size-acceptance training to professionals and other groups.

OTHER WHOLE PERSON PRODUCTS

WORKING WITH GROUPS
TO OVERCOME PANIC, ANXIETY, & PHOBIAS
Shirley Babior, LCSW, MFCC, and Carol Goldman, LICSW

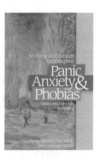

Written especially for therapists, this manual presents well-researched, state-of-the-art treatment strategies for a variety of anxiety disorders. It includes treatment goals, basic anxiety-recovery exercises, and recovery enhancers that encourage lifestyle changes. Sessions in this manual are related directly to the chapters in **Overcoming Panic, Anxiety, & Phobias**.

❑ **Working with Groups to Overcome Panic, Anxiety, & Phobias / $24.95**
❑ **Worksheet Masters / $9.95**

OVERCOMING PANIC, ANXIETY, & PHOBIAS
Shirley Babior, LCSW, MFCC, and Carol Goldman, LICSW

For people who suffer from panic disorder, anxiety issues, or phobias, this practical self-help guide provides concrete advice as well as hopeful personal stories of recovery. Tips include managing catastrophic thoughts with rational responses, facing fearful situations, dealing with setbacks, and using relaxation to reduce physical symptoms.

❑ **Overcoming Panic, Anxiety, & Phobias / $12.95**

COMPANION AUDIOTAPES:
❑ **Calm Down:** Relaxation and Imagery Skills for Managing Stress, Anxiety, and Panic / $11.95
❑ **Worry Stoppers:** Breathing and Imagery to Calm the Restless Mind / $11.95

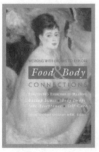

WORKING WITH GROUPS TO EXPLORE
FOOD & BODY CONNECTIONS
Sandy Stewart Christian, MSW, Editor

This innovative collection of 36 group processes gathered from experts around the country tackles complex and painful issues nearly everyone is concerned aboutó dieting, weight, healthy eating, fitness, body image, and self-esteemóusing a whole person approach that advocates health and fitness for people of all sizes.

Move beyond diets and weight management with this essential tool for wellness educators, therapists, dieticians, nurses, trainers, program planners, and other health professionals.

❑ **Working with Groups to Explore Food & Body Connections / $24.95**
❑ **Worksheet Masters / $9.95**

COMPANION AUDIOTAPES:
❑ **Body Image:** Affirming Meditations for People of All SIzes / $11.95
❑ **Eating:** Guided Imagery for Making Peace with Food / $11.95

© 1997 Whole Person Associates 210 W Michigan Duluth, MN 55802   (800) 247-6789

OTHER WHOLE PERSON PRODUCTS

WORKING WITH WOMENíS GROUPS
Volumes 1 & 2
Louise Yolton Eberhardt

The two volumes of **Working with Womenís Groups** have been completely revised and updated. **Volume 1** explores consciousness raising, self-discovery, and assertiveness training. **Volume 2** looks at sexuality issues, women of color, and leadership skills training.

❑ **Working with Womenís Groups**
  Volumes 1 & 2 / $24.95 per volume

❑ **Worksheet Masters**
  Volumes 1 & 2 / $9.95 per volume

WORKING WITH MENíS GROUPS
Roger Karsk and Bill Thomas

Working with Menís Groups has been updated to reflect the reality of menís lives in the 1990s. Each exercise follows a structured pattern to help trainers develop either onetime workshops or ongoing groups that explore menís issues in four key areas: self-discovery, consciousness raising, intimacy, and parenting.

❑ **Working with Menís Groups / $24.95**
❑ **Worksheet Masters / $9.95**

WORKING WITH GROUPS FROM DYSFUNCTIONAL FAMILIES
Cheryl Hetherington

Even the healthiest family can be dysfunctional at times, making everyone vulnerable to the pain of difficult family relationships.

This collection of 29 proven group activities is designed to heal the pain that results from living in a dysfunctional family. With these exercises leaders can promote healing, build self-esteem, encourage sharing, and help participants acknowledge their feelings.

❑ **Working with Groups from Dysfunctional Families / $24.95**
❑ **Worksheet Masters / $9.95**